Love, Sex, and Other Things You Might Find At The Airport

By Zaron Burnett III

Thought Catalog

Love, Sex, and Other Things You Might Find At The Airport

A THOUGHT CATALOG ORIGINAL

© 2013 Zaron Burnett III

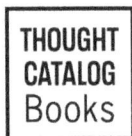

THOUGHT CATALOG
Books

Copyright © 2018 by The Thought & Expression Co. All rights reserved. Published by Thought Catalog Books, a publishing house owned by The Thought & Expression Co., Williamsburg, Brooklyn. Second edition, 2018.

ISBN 978-1-945796-64-7

Cover Photo: © iStockPhoto.com/yulkapopkova
Cover Design: www.athleticsnyc.com

Does Hollywood Make Romantic Comedies Just To Fuck With Us?

T his morning I woke up in bed alone. If you're lucky enough not to remember what that's like, it totally sucked. I hate waking up in bed alone. I'd sell one of my kidneys on the black market if somehow it would guarantee I'd find my one true love and get to spend the rest of my days and nights and mornings with her. But that's my fucking problem. I believe in imaginary things like "true love." I don't blame my divorced parents or Disney fairytales or even the American public school system. There's only one destructive, corrupting force I blame–those beautiful lies we call romantic comedies. They made me this way. Unlike Lady Gaga, I wasn't born this way. I was born cynical. But after years of training, I succumbed to their lessons of love and romance. I want a fast-talking woman to shake up my whole world.

I dislike the term manic pixie dream girl-I never wanted one of those. But the screwball heroines could do no wrong in my eyes. And because of them I always gaze around at the baggage claim at the airport with the stupid hope I'll have some meet-cute with a sexy and slightly daffy smart woman and start a life-changing love story. They're also why I'll wake up in bed alone again tomorrow. And it'll be difficult not to wonder, *"Does Hollywood make romantic comedies just to fuck with us?"*

Ernst Lubitsch, Billy Wilder, Howard Hawks, Neil Simon, Woody Allen, Peter Bogdanovich (but only for *What's Up Doc?)*, John Hughes, Nora Ephron, Cameron Crowe, Richard Curtis, James L. Brooks, and David O. Russell.

These twelve sadists ruined me. Their funny, smart dialog, their cynicism clinging to whatever romance it could hold, their tough, funny heroines and awkward, irreverent heroes, all combined to show me how love was before I ever experienced it. They made fake love look so good that real love never stood a chance.

Romantic comedies seem inconsequential, about as meaningful as pop love songs of the Sixties. That's how their particular brand of brainwashing works. Romantic comedies are like delicately decorated cupcakes. They seem mostly harmless. At worst a guilty treat. But how does the saying go, "A moment on the lips... a lifetime on the hips?" Rom-coms spend a lifetime on the hips of your mind. For the rest of your life those characters will whisper ideas of what love feels like and the scenes will give you visual references of what romance looks like.

Studies show that when we watch movies and television our brains process the experience on many levels, and at the motor skills level thanks to mirror neuron cells, we subconsciously feel as if we're going through the experiences of the actors onscreen. Which suggests everyone ought to worry about the influence of action movies and horror films. Yet those movies never make me want to punch anyone in the throat. It was the romantic comedies that fucked me up and no one ever worried they were warping my young mind. Action movies never looked real, but the love stories looked enough like real life that I believed them. And that's when you're doomed.

When I was a little boy, I turned every stick into a gun. And now, as an adult, I turn every romance in my life into a two-person Hollywood movie because apparently, my stupid brain thought that shit was real. If I was more paranoid or dramatic about such things I would claim romantic comedies brainwashed me. But that would be ridiculous.

The trouble is, in the real world, if you use rom-coms as inspiration you're just as likely to end up coming off as desperate as you're likely to persuade someone to give you a shot. What looks cool blown up to 35 feet and projected onscreen, doesn't always feel the same when it's focused at a real person. There's a word for using the rom-com approach: overkill. Nothing kills sexiness faster than *overkill*. The dudes of romantic comedies detonate any sense of proportion. In real life they'd seem maudlin, neurotic, anxious, diffident, self-conscious, pretentious, obsessive and more in love with the idea of love than love itself, especially the guys in teen romantic comedies. Yeah, I'm looking at you John Cusack, Freddie Prinze Jr. and Michael Cera. Rom-com dudes like those three distort expectations. If you ever find you're thinking and talking like Lloyd Dobler, or you wish Llody Dobler was in your life... huge red flag. I know this personal doom. No good comes from measuring your love with celluloid.

For an ex-girlfriend's birthday I planned a whole day as a surprise. Our day started with homemade breakfast, but not in bed because she didn't like breakfast in bed. I didn't tell her where we were going or what we were doing. I suggested she wear a sundress, bring sunglasses and maybe a sweater. She liked surprises, somewhat. And she got excited when I told her we were going for a drive. We both loved road trips. I burned a series of mix CDs, rather than create a giant iPod playlist, that way each mix CD was its own musical statement. Seemed more romantic.

We were lucky. We loved each other, but we were also friends, which is super-important for a road trip. We drove south from San Francisco down the Pacific Coast Highway. It's one of those drives you've seen in countless car commercials since you were a kid. It's a strip of blacktop running along the edge of the continent, separated from the ocean by a cliff. The views are all eye-candy. And that day, the ocean looked like it had been photoshopped. It was impossibly blue-green beautiful. Fuzzy fingers of clouds reached across the sky. My girlfriend enjoyed the drive. And loved the music. We talked for long stretches after each mix CD ended. She kept grinning.

I'd planned little deviations along the way. We stopped at a redwood grove and took a walk amongst the silent giants. I made the mistake of mentioning I'd been to the grove of tall trees before to attend a friend's Nordic Wiccan wedding ceremony. I think this gave her ideas of where our walk was leading, but in all honesty, I had no destination other than to circle back to the car. I'd loaded the day down with so much romance, my ex-girlfriend started to believe it was the sort of day she'd need to remember for the rest of her life. I just wanted her to have a cool birthday and overshot my target by half.

My ex-girlfriend looked sexy stomping up the trail, lit by the sunlight streaking through the trees, and I told her so. I guess our walk in the redwoods and the way her dress sashayed back and forth against her legs started to turn her on. She told me this later because, like a true rom-com hero, I missed the signs. She stopped at a little bend in the trail at the peak of a small hill. Wanting to make sure she had a perfect birthday I checked the time and saw we'd be cutting it close to make our reservations, so I suggested we head back to the car. She'd stopped because she wanted to have a quickie beneath the canopy of redwoods on the cool of that soft fern-covered earth. Too much of a lady to mention this, she said nothing; until later, when she laughed about how I totally missed the signs on that one. You see how scripted rom-com plans of romance cause you to miss out on the truly important things in life... like sneaking off for some outdoor sex?

There was a really exclusive and expensive resort in the middle of Big Sur and I'd heard they had a beautiful cliff-top restaurant and anyone could make reservations without being a guest of the resort, which is exactly what I did. She loved the view. The food was the sort you'd remember and compare later meals to. We drank champagne and toasted to her birthday. We ordered desert and enjoyed the view as the sun sank into the Pacific. She loved her day of surprises.

Sometimes a woman will smile and it looks like it almost hurts her, like she can't stop smiling, and her face pains her with a persistent widespread grin. My girlfriend was beaming so brightly I thought she might start crying. What I didn't know was I'd just ruined our relationship forever.

I wanted to give her an awesome birthday but what I'd just told her in the subtext of the day was I loved her and wanted to be with her forever. This is rom-com overkill. I sent a way stronger message than I intended. And it ruined everything. She thought we were getting married and started judging everything against that eventual goal.

Critics love to accuse rom-coms of being sexist, conservative propaganda based on the same "princess fantasy" that's existed for centuries. Like that's such a clever indictment. Of course they are! We happily pay good money to see some of that fake love and false hope. Love stories make us stupid. And we love them for it. Never forget, ignorance is bliss. And "love conquers all" is one of the more ignorant statements ever uttered. But to see it play out is pure bliss for some folks.

Our modern Western notions of love and romance date back to the Middle Ages. They were spread by the troubadours of Occitan whose song-poems celebrated the joy and pains of love. Their work popularized stories of knights, chivalry, unrequited love, damsels-in-distress, and the unmediated grandeur of "true love." They're the assholes that put romance up on its pedestal. Before them love marriages were a luxury of the very lucky and very wealthy. Everyone else married some bloke on the block or gal in the village and that was that. What made the romances of the troubadours so epic, so memorable, so lasting, were all the great obstacles to love. Obstacles are sexy to our imaginations. And sadly, this is also why my ex-girlfriend hung in there even after I told her I didn't want to get married. She thought, just like how it all works out in the third act of a movie, she'd wear me down, and in the end her love would conquer my doubts. You'll notice that didn't happen, since she's my ex-girlfriend.

Far as I can tell, real love is the creation of something greater than your self. That's it in a snapshot. And embracing the "greater-than-yourself" ideal is what old school romantic comedies did so well. These days, Hollywood's a little clumsy with the key that turns a good love story. They seem to forget that just as superheroes sacrifice it all to save the world, young lovers sacrifice it all for love, because at that moment, love is their whole world. And how they sacrifice it all offers the lessons we enjoy with laughs and tears and hopefully we exit with some increased understanding. These days, Hollywood makes rom-coms like they're advertisements designed to sell you love. And the films are about as meaningful as perfume ads.

The best rom-coms are always equal parts myth, fairytale, and self-help book. And for years now, I thought they were fucking with me. But I guess that's like blaming McDonald's for making someone obese. No one has to eat at McDonald's. And Hollywood isn't really fucking with me, or you. I decided to let the films run amok in my imagination and stomp all over my heart. And using rom-com romance in real life is like watering your houseplants with a fire hose. It took me awhile to learn that. People won't understand, or maybe won't trust, your expressions of love if they're too romantic. In real life, we need imperfection. Real love is messy, sloppy, tongue-tied, and it stops for an afternoon quickie. We can't plan love. We can't script love. We just have to show up. That's what real love is all about-being alive and present for another person.

It's too late for me. Rom-coms will forever keep me looking for love at airports and train stations and flea markets and produce sections of grocery stores. But at least now, I show up without a script because I'm sick of waking up alone. Maybe instead of a kidney, if I give up my celluloid daydreams of love, I'll find a real woman to share my days and nights and mornings. Turns out,

Hollywood doesn't give a shit about us. It isn't fucking with us. We just need to stop fucking with ourselves.

* *

Strangers Are Often The Sexiest People You'll Meet

A friend of mine introduced me to John Money's sexual theory that borrows cartography as a metaphor for your erotic inner world. He called it a "Lovemap." My friend is interested in the aesthetics of bondage and kink. And in her studies and reading she came across this rather eloquent way to chart the full continent of your sexuality and all the numerous ways you might find arousal. It seems most poor souls don't fully explore all of the rivers and streams, lakes and valleys of what gets them to say,"Ohmyfuckin' Gawd! Yess!" This is a mistake. One we should all avoid.

Why live a life deprived of such pleasure? People used to save themselves for marriage. Or at least pretended they did. They grew up and rarely left their hometown. They were stuck in the rut of one culture and often with one person's (or at most, a handful of people's) turn-ons and turn-offs. Now we have jet airplanes and birth control which means you should taste many cultures of the world and have as many one-night stands as you think proper and good for you. I mean it. We should all explore the boundary-lands of our personal lovemaps.

Obviously, married people, you'll have to do your exploring on the old homefront. Unless you're into polyamory, and if so, then jump on in the hottub. Now, I don't intend to sound like I am, or share values with, some cheesy pick-up artist. Nor do I wish to borrow the attitude of certain lubricant-greased libertines who suggest everyone should be fucking more. I just think everyone should be fucking more. The three of us all happen to agree on that basic point.

And if the truth were spoken, we *all* agree on that point, *right*? Except of course, those of you in the asexual community. And I'd never suggest anyone from your community should feel the need to have sex, or feel pressured about sex. But the rest of you, that's exactly what I'm saying. You should have more sex. And make it more creative sex. Together, let's make one-night stands frequent and classy again. I'm not sure they were ever classy, or even frequent, except maybe in the Seventies but that included a lot of polyester and cocaine, two great tastes that did not taste great together.

Here's the idea, go find a sexy stranger, take them to a warm place and do delicious things. Try shit your last girlfriend or ex-boyfriend never wanted to do. Let the stranger handcuff you, blindfold you and beat you with a riding crop and then lick powdered honey off your body where your skin is still hot and red from the sting of the crop. Or do that shit to them. And also do silly things, like eat that fruit roll-up stuff they call edible underwear. Do free-spirited things, like go fuck on a rooftop in a major metropolitan area in the middle of the day. Or in a public park while every one else is watching the Fourth of July fireworks. Get yourself some of that hair-pulling, skin-biting, nail-scratching, intense sort of sex with a stranger you barely know. Enjoy fucking the way Grandma and Grandpa never had a chance to... because you owe it to them to get naked and explore another person's turn-ons and turn-offs. And they'd want you to. You might learn something about yourself. Exploration of another person is also self-exploration.

I once took a girl home just to find out if she was a man or a woman. I know what you're probably thinking... *Why the hell would you do that?* Well, there is no good reason. I'm just terribly curious. And she was sexy even if I couldn't tell what she was packing in her panties. You see, I was in West Hollywood and some friends and I were at the Rainbow Room up on the Sunset Strip. It's in WeHo but it's not a gay bar, it's a somewhat famous/infamous rocker bar. While we were celebrating my friend's birthday this gal in a polka-dot dress came up to me-and she was a big woman. She had hands as big as mine and I rarely meet men with hands as large as mine. But yet there was something sexy about her I found fascinating. Might've been the combination of her smile and the way she spread those polka dots. When she suggested we go back to her place, I just nodded. As we left together my friends looked at me like I was crazy. Again, I just nodded and then waved goodbye.

She drove a lifted black truck with flames on the mud-flaps. Kinda suggested she was a dude. But while she drove us back to her place she told me how she worked construction and never did anything like this, and how she was shy but she felt very aroused for some reason when she saw me. I liked that neither of us knew exactly the reason we were doing this. It just needed to happen, I guess. While we stole through the night, the skeptical and suspicious parts of me teamed up and suggested to my imagination that when we got to her place there'd probably be a group of Satanists waiting there. Or she was a guy. The jury was still out.

When we arrived at her place I was damn glad to find out I was wrong. No Satanists. And she had a very feminine apartment. She changed into a skimpy little negligee. Since she was about six-feet tall it didn't really cover much. She looked like Marilyn Monroe... if Marilyn was a starting middle linebacker in the NFL. She had broad shoulders, I assumed from swinging a hammer for a living. And I still couldn't tell if she was a dude or not. The first thing I noticed was she had 118 pictures of Jesus on her walls. I know this because I counted. When I asked her why so many pics of her Lord and savior she told me about the multiple car accidents she'd survived and how one of her feet had once been sewn back on to her leg. Seems she'd had a tough life. We smoked a joint and listened to music and then started making out like high school kids, drunk and awkwardly on the couch.

Much to my surprise I discovered not only was she definitely a woman, she was a very passionate woman who was clearly under-appreciated because how big she was. In her bedroom, underneath roughly another 31 pictures of Jesus, we fucked until the sun came up and we'd drained her supply of condoms. Despite her rough construction worker hands and her broad shoulders and rather mannish size we moved with coordinated rhythms and enjoyed the small hours of the early morning, stress-testing her bed. It left me practically unable to walk the next morning.

Now, this may not be your idea of a good time but my curiosity and my willingness to go where apparently not many other men dared to go offered me the rare chance to enjoy the pleasure of a woman yearning to be satisfied. And from some place deep inside her she opened up a fountain of sexuality that left us both wet, spent and sore in a way I've yet to experience again.

In spite of my enthusiastic endorsement of full tilt sexuality, I don't want to confuse you. I don't mean for you to go out and try things you aren't comfortable with, only things you're curious about. If unlike Rihanna whips and chains don't excite you... don't go stupid crazy with S&M. Don't let someone talk you into a group sex situation if you've never been the least bit curious about what a room full of writhing sweaty bodies feels like. That's not for you. But if you always wanted to join the Mile High Club and some sexy stranger seduces you on a cross-country flight, then, like a certain shoe company has suggested for years... *Just fucking do it!*

One-night stands can be supremely wonderful experiences. But you'll fuck yourself up, if you go into it requiring false tenderness. For chrissakes, it's a one-night stand! A good and sexy one-night stand should be very physical, super-exciting, an almost primal exhaustion of your sexual imagination, but most certainly not a lie of intimacy. Save real intimacy for your girlfriend, your boyfriend, your long-time lovers, husbands and wives. They deserve your intimacy. A one-night stand requires your lusty imagination. Life is short and to be savored like fresh-made ice cream on a hot summer day. Let life run down your arm and stain your clothing.

If you go about a one-night stand the wrong way it can be horrible and you will feel like how preachers and moralists warn you will feel. Done wrong, it's like masturbating with another person's body. And they will leave you feeling more empty or alone when you wake up and crawl home. The key to avoiding a truly bad one-night stand is honesty and decency. You probably didn't expect me to say that. But, it's true. Always use common decency.

It's much better if you consider the other person's feelings and spend the night together. Don't just hop up and leave when you're done. Then in the morning, you can avoid the awkwardness of waking up together, sober, puffy-faced and needing a toothbrush, by having a sense of humor about the whole thing. No one looks particularly great the morning after. Although, I do imagine Astrid

Berges-Frisbey looks pretty tremendous when she wakes up. But she's French. They have an unfair advantage when it comes to looking beautiful when tousled. French guys and girls both know how to pull off messy-sexy.

One of the greatest benefits of adulthood is you live by your own rules. You judge yourself by your own morality. Please, don't take your parents and church to bed with you. You're both (or, you're all) adults. As long as you respect your partner(s), and you know what you're doing, a one-night stand is a great way to feel dirty, sexy and alive. Even though it's just one night, or one long weekend, enjoy some orgasms with strangers. It's like giving Death the middle finger. Orgasms are the biological reward for trying to pass our genes forward. It's a small defiant victory in our losing battle against death. A good and proper one-night stand is born of your acceptance of adult decisions and it's a vital reminder of your fleeting time on Earth. Pursue the borders of your lovemap. Get out there and... get to fucking!

* *

Romance Isn't Dead… It's Just Not Speaking To Any Of Us

W hen was the last time you went out on a date? Like a real date with romance and spontaneity, something you might tell your friends about and they all say, "Awww! I wish that happened to me?" Or if you're a guy, "Fuck, dude. That sounds awesome." If you're under thirty, I'd be willing to bet it's been a long time, if ever. Why is that? When did romance become the walking dead of clichés? Has modern life made us all so cynical that romance is as played out as poodle skirts? I'm a fan of romance, of little surprises, of taking the time to find some unexpected spots to take a gal and show her a good time that'll become warm memories and make her feel like the princess I think she is. Now, don't get me wrong-I don't think women are weak, sentimental creatures who should be put on a pedestal and worshipped, nor do I think they're delicate little things one must handle like paper flowers. I just believe that it's fun to show a woman that she's special. Way too often a woman receives the opposite message from a rather cruel and indifferent world. They're convinced through repetition of the message they're not special and they shouldn't expect anyone to go out of their way to give them some smiles and moments that make their heart flutter. I think that's bullshit.

If you can't tell already, I like taking someone's breath away. It doesn't always work well for me because apparently, I'm now in the minority. Lots of women think I'm "too thoughtful" and that either I'm some smooth-talking player who's just doing the dance to get in their pants-or worse-I'm a "nice guy." I may be kind but I'm no "nice guy." I'll tell a woman when I think she's acting selfishly. I know where my boundaries are. I don't take shovel-loads of shit in the vain hope a woman will get naked with me. But I cherish women and sadly this is somehow a negatively perceived trait. I don't know what other dudes are doing out there in the dating world but I have to believe there are plenty of guys like me. And if you are one don't let the world wear you down. Don't have any shame in your game. Romance is one of the coolest ways to spend your time.

Rather than ask why others don't value it, for those of us who appreciate it, the question is: How does one romance the one they want in a world that mistrusts those who still believe in making an extra effort to show that special someone that their smile is more valuable than gold? Like with most things that truly matter in this life... *you gotta do you.* This is a mantra people toss around but few have the eggs or the balls to really let it determine all their decisions.

First, commit. Really and truly commit to being the sort of guy or gal you want to be, even if that means you're misunderstood. If someone doesn't get it-then that means they don't get it and you should move on. Other folks will learn to trust romance is something that matters to you and they'll open up and learn to appreciate it, savor it and enjoy the little things you do. And maybe, just maybe, you'll get lucky and meet someone who was raised to appreciate the dance of romance.

Before we get too far down the road to love... What is romance? When I use that word I don't mean it the way pick-up artists mean it. It's not a competition, nor is it a game to win someone over. Instead, it's a way to show someone how their happiness is your happiness, too. It's a way to give them goosebumps in that good-good way. It's a language of lovers that outsiders don't have to understand.

When I was a boy, I learned from men how to romance a woman. As a teenager, I watched movies that gave me a few extra pointers. The key is integrity. You have to really mean what you say, what you write, what you do. And the other critical component is to listen. Let the small voice inside you whisper good ideas. Pay attention to the person you desire, in small throwaway moments of life, she or he will often give you clues about what matters to them. And when they do remember them like they're a combination to the safe that is their heart.

Romance is light like flower petals. It's fun like running through sprinklers. It's simple like a walk on an empty beach at sunset. It's funny like a day trip to a petting zoo. It's tender like a fresh honeydew melon you brought for a picnic in a park. The key to romance is what you're doing is for someone else not for you. Don't do it to score points. Don't do it because you think it's a panty-dropper. That's using romance like a tool. It's not a can-opener. You should do it because you want them to feel how you feel about them.

As I pointed out romance these days has a bad rep, it's considered cliché. We're all so busy being ironic there's no room for romance, the earnestness of romance looks childish and naïve. Possibly even needy. What a sad pitiful lot we are, the ones who prefer vague stances to slow dances. I say fuck all that noise. You wanna know what's a very common modern cliché? Being a self-absorbed, self-motivated, selfish sonofabitch who always wants to know what's in it for them. Romance is the exact opposite instinct. It asks what's in it for the other. It takes the focus off of you and places your attention on the one you love. It relieves you of the burdens of your boundaries. It frees you to celebrate someone other than yourself.

If you struggle with conceiving ways to romance someone, study what others have done and then make their ways your own. Read poetry. Watch romantic movies and romantic comedies (be careful with this). Be careful not to over do it. Like with music, less is more. What's better than consulting movies would be to talk to anyone over the age of seventy and then they'll give you a wealth of ideas of what true romance looks and feels like. And throw out the notion it's about money. You can be romantic for free. It's time and effort that make romance valuable. The notion you're carrying them around with you and thinking of them when they're not around is the message that comes through when you surprise them with something special.

Take them to a museum on the free day, because almost every museum has one free day a month. Take a walk and enjoy the fall foliage, or the spring blossoms, or the smells of summer, or the whiteness of winter. Make a home-cooked meal they once mentioned they've always wanted to try. Surprise them with a song you wrote, or a love letter, or a drawing, or just a little note slipped into their purse or pocket.

When you spread romance, when you let love lead, when you express what you feel without fear or limitation you urge who you care about to come out and play, and that's what we all want and need, someone who loves us, wants the best for us, and makes our world a funnier, more lively, laughing, playful, smiling place to live and love. These days, the world moves so fast everything quickly becomes a cliché. And if you're gonna be a cliché, why not be the cliché who's in love?

* *

What's Up With Lena Dunham? (Celebrating Real Women's Bodies)

I n Los Angeles you spend time at gas stations like New Yorkers wait for subways. One of the perks though, if you like to eavesdrop like I do, L.A. gas stations are the great social equalizers. Everyone needs gas, from celebrities to lost tourists. Recently, I listened to two young women critically discuss the show, *Girls*.

The tall one wondered, "What's up with Lena Dunham? Why does she always wanna get naked? Does she think it makes the show better? That like... people wanna see *that*? Or is she just making a point–it's her show and she has *the power*–she can do whatever she wants? Is she like just some girl with a bad body getting back at all the beautiful girls?"

So much going on with that series of questions. I wanted to ask them if we could all go get some coffee and discuss it. But I knew that'd probably sound really weird. And I didn't have the time anyway. Still, I kept thinking about what she said.

"What's up with Lena Dunham? Why does she always wanna get naked?"

I suppose only Ms. Dunham knows the answer to that one.

"Does she think it makes the show better?"

Don't think that's her entire motivation to drop her dress so often.

"That like... people wanna see *that*?"

This one really caught my ear. It was the word "*that*." She really loaded up that single syllable. She weighed it down with so much judgment I felt bad for the little pronoun. She was obviously referring to way more than nudity. She was critical of Ms. Dunham's body. But she didn't linger, she moved on to the question of power.

"Or is she just making a point–it's her show and she has *the power*-she can do whatever she wants?"

This was the key turning point. I don't think she realized all the feminist arguments she was raising about a woman having the power to bare her body before the world and do so on her terms, on her show, and be the subject of her own "gaze," since Ms. Dunham is often the director of the episodes when she gets naked.

But then the young woman swerved back to the critical question at hand...

"Is she like just some girl with a bad body getting back at all the beautiful girls?"

Rather than discuss Lena Dunham's power, this young woman was far more interested in evaluating her attractiveness, seeing her as someone who dared to "get back at all the beautiful girls" of the world. I couldn't tell if she thought this was a good thing. Or if it was an act of folly, like a mere mortal challenging the Greek gods. I never found out because the next thing she said was, "Fifty on twelve."

Then she and her friend left the gas station. Yet her words stayed with me and left me wondering for hours... "What's up with Lena Dunham?"

The sexiness and the beauty of a woman are often confused as the same thing. But they're not. Sexiness is a swirl of physical attractiveness and attitude. And it's entirely subjective. Beauty is an appreciation of uniqueness. It can be considered objectively, like how we discuss art. Often a majority of people will agree on the beauty of a thing or a person. Which means it doesn't matter if you think Lena Dunham is sexy or not... but anyone can say she's beautiful (which she is).

People get so excited about boobs and vaginas. And I don't just mean men and boys. Women do, too. I've noticed women often grow anxious when confronted with female nudity. Not because it's indecent but because it can trigger their own insecurities. From what I understand, female insecurities about their bodies are, sadly, about as common as mosquitos in Mississippi.

It's a shame we've turned beauty into such a rigid standard it's now a nightclub few can get in. It's depressing that so many women suffer their whole lives because of it. From girlhood to the grave most women never feel they measure up. They look in the mirror and see all kinds of wrong. They isolate areas and zones of their body they hate. They criticize themselves for their collection of imperfections.

My sister grew up hating how she looked. I saw how much she struggled to like herself because of it. She was convinced she was fat. She wasn't. She was just curvier and more muscular than most the other girls in our hometown. None of that mattered. In the mirror, all she saw was a heifer.

I didn't understand how deeply held her belief was until high school. We were arguing about some "bitch at school" calling her fat. I argued my sister wasn't fat. I said the other girl was an asshole and just trying to hurt her feelings. We kept arguing. I got frustrated. And said to myself-*Fuck it. I'm sick of arguing about her being fat.* So, I tried agreeing with her. I said I could see how the "bitch from school" might think she was fat but it didn't matter what the bitch thought.

I know... that was pretty much the stupidest things I could've said.

I didn't say she was fat. I said I could see why someone would say that. No matter how many times I told her she was beautiful, no matter how many times I argued she wasn't fat, because I uttered this one statement I confirmed all her deepest fears she was a heifer.

To this day she remembers that moment. And I've regretted it. From the second the words left my lips and I saw her eyes change, until now, I've regretted it. But the damage was done. That's how I learned about how deep it goes and why so many women struggle against the female beauty ideal. It's some hardcore shit.

For my sister, my young niece, and all the women who suffer from body image anxiety, I'm stoked Lena Dunham is on television dropping her dress and that she has the power to confront the tyranny of the female beauty ideal. I'm also stoked she's not alone. There's a growing trend of art and media projects celebrating real women's bodies. Right now, there's a wave of images of everyday women washing over our culture, crumbling the sandcastles dedicated to the reigning ideas of beauty.

Importantly, these authentic images of real women's bodies aren't about women being sexy. They're not about what men like or want to see. These images of nudity are all about the beauty of women and offer them a way to see each other's bodies and feel better about themselves.

If a woman must compare herself, and it does seem to be natural to compare, at least now she can compare herself to other real human beings. For far too long our media has undermined women with false images. How could anyone live up to such an unrealistic ideal? Women are doomed from the start. The female beauty ideal is the Original Sin that corrupts what women believe about their bodies. It's way too easy to forget the man-made images are make-upped, photoshopped, airbrushed creations. They're totally unreal. It's like a horse comparing itself to a unicorn.

The NU Project is a photo-project created by, Matt Blum, a Minneapolis-based photographer, and his wife Katy Kessler. They ask everyday women to pose nude in their own homes. The photos celebrate real women's bodies in their natural environment. He uses the same techniques one would use for a fashion model shoot. Good lighting, beautiful composition, inspired poses and an attitude of intimacy. The photos capture each woman's individual beauty.

Additionally, on Tumblr, there are other projects designed to free women from the anxiety of wondering if they're normal. If you're looking for female nudity, Tumblr is a good place to start. However, separate from the the usual nude selfies, screen captures of porn films, and wild-ass hentai, there are two Tumblr pages dedicated to exploding the female beauty ideal. One features large labia and the other catalogs breasts of all sizes. A young woman named Emma created the two spaces specifically for women. Internet spelunker and Tumblr curator, Dora Moutot, the French artist responsible for *Webcam Tears*, made me aware of both projects.

OurBreasts is a curated collection devoted to celebrating the many shapes, sizes and colors of breasts. For young girls and women who feel self-conscious, the variety of breasts on display answer the question, "Am I normal?" Women submit photos and write testimonials of their struggles with self-acceptance and the doubt that bedevils each new generation of women.

Emma's other page, *LargeLabiaProject*, is a Tumblr photo gallery of selfies of vaginas. If I were embarrassed about my labia, this would be a great site to visit. Some folks have argued the project reinforces the stigma because it inversely suggests large labia are unusual and women must be told they're normal.

As a kid, I never liked hearing someone tell me, "A black man was the first person to perform open heart surgery." I always thought, "So what? Does that surprise you?" So I understand the value-inversion argument, however, in this instance I think the testimonials on the site suggest a more important dynamic at work.

One visitor wrote, "You should know how very much this has helped me. I am a young woman in her 20's and I implore you to continue... if one day a girl who is insecure and worried stumbles across this project as opposed to a link for labiaplasty then you have made a large difference. Wish I had. We as women so often self mutilate and this is a thing that can be changed."

Her regret articulates how a few inches of skin and tissue can turn into years of shame and suffering, and drive a woman to seek out unnecessary surgery to fix what's wrong. There's nothing wrong with a woman's labia or any other part of her body. To quote Jane's Addiction, "Ain't no wrong now... ain't no right."

Even if you think you're overweight, underweight, pockmarked, stretch-marked, wrinkled, or lumpy, you're as beautiful as a giraffe. And yes, I know it's lame to compare a woman to an animal. But I think just this once we can drop any charges of sexism since I'm comparing all of us to giraffes. We're all animals... just talking monkeys who learned to shave our legs and faces.

That's what the young woman in the gas station forgot. Lena Dunham doesn't have a bad body. She has a human body. Since we're just animals, she has a body as beautiful as a swan and no one criticizes a swan for being naked.

And it's awesome that Lena Dunham is another voice joining the growing chorus of women overcoming anxiety, women rushing past the outmoded beauty ideals. Together, naked as jaybirds, they're loudly singing, "Real women's bodies are beautiful! Totally fucking beautiful!"

* *

The Way You Do Anything Is The Way You Do Everything

H ow do you feel about doing the little things in life? Don't know about you but I absolutely, fundamentally hate to do laundry. Like any normal person, I reserve most of my hatred for reprehensible things like child slavery, sex trafficking, and Donald Trump's stupid ass. But if there are still any loathsome feelings left over I apply them to my laundry. Despite my irrational hatred for it, I just did all my laundry. Not surprisingly, I feel way better. Not like orgasmic but it's better than existential ennui.

Why is it so easy to forget the good feelings we gain by doing the little things in life?

Why do we tend to ignore the little voice inside that reminds us what we need to do? Or really, should do.

Do we all resent authority so much that even when it's just the little voice inside of us we tend to ignore it?

Maybe you don't. But I should listen more because I usually forget how good clean laundry feels. Every week it slips from memory. For some silly reason, I have trouble keeping in mind how little things like clean laundry actually make a huge difference. Perhaps I need to get a tattoo to remind me: *Do the little things, Jackass!*

You might've heard someone say: **You are your truest self when nobody is looking.**

In the moments when you're alone, when there's nothing to gain or risk socially, when there's no one to impress, no one to scold or shame you, that's when you can see who you are as plain as the sun in the sky. There's no denying or rationalizing how you behave when you're alone. There's no one around to secretly blame, no one to motivate you to do what you must. Those dishes in the sink are like an accusatory finger. If you had company coming over they wouldn't still be there. That would be embarrassing. But since it's just you... you can always wash them later. Yet the unspoken question remains: *Doesn't your environment matter? Aren't you as important as your guests?*

In order to enjoy some life in my home I keep cacti and other succulent plants. They're not my favorite plants but they can live for weeks without water. It's hard to kill a cactus. Of course... I've done it. But it takes time. You don't need to watch me slow-kill a houseplant to know maintenance isn't my thing. All you'd need to see is my attitude towards laundry and there's no denying I suck at doing those terribly necessary things we call life maintenance. The fact I dislike laundry means I also forget about oil changes. You see? It's the same choice disguised by details. There's an invisible connection between the two. And it's the same for you-any one choice you make resembles all your other choices.

Buying cacti and keeping them alive is helping me to remember to do my laundry, which helps me remember to change my oil, which helps me remember to buy groceries on a regular basis. Each choice ripples and makes it easier to make other smart choices. Basically, not killing a cactus means I eat better.

If you have a few things about yourself you'd like to change, behaviors you'd like to adopt, bad habits you'd like to drop, it doesn't matter if it's a big thing like quitting smoking, losing weight, learning to save money, or just a small thing like remembering to do your laundry, here's a little secret that'll help you find the courage, the diligence, the motivation, the stick-to-it-ness necessary to change. And trust me I know because I need the reminder probably more than you do.

The secret is: ***Don't focus on the thing you want to change.***

With such tight tunnel vision you can be easily overcome by negative thinking. You psychologically compound the situation when you obsessively fixate on what you wish to change. Every time you fail to change you beat yourself up a little more. Instead of focusing on that one negative thing, enlarge your gaze and pay attention to how you do everything. Find ways to constantly win tiny battles.

If you want to remember to do your laundry, make sure you floss. Value your health and wellbeing throughout your life. If you want to quit smoking, start playing softball. It helps you make healthier choices if they're fun. If you want to want to lose weight, don't start some crazy strict diet that makes you say no to yourself all the time. That's horseshit. Instead, go find a pool and start swimming regularly, or if a bathing suit makes you feel awkward, pick an activity you enjoy doing that gets you up and moving and you'll see how much easier it is to make new food choices. Your general attitude will shift from negative obsession to positive gain. You'll naturally shift your priorities.

Experts say that after 90 days or so making new choices, they unconsciously become new habits. You pick a new way to move through the world. And as you benefit from the resulting good feelings and confidence, those old bad behaviors/old habits, your poor choices, they fall away like dead leaves in autumn.

The underlying idea is: ***The way you do anything is the way you do everything.***

It's pretty simple when you get right down to it. You have a way you move through the world. It's observable in everything you do. And as much as it can help you see yourself clearly, you can also understand others. If you're the sort who's often mislead by others, it helps you see them clearly, if you pay attention to them without trying to see anything. Just watch what someone does. And how they do it. With a little practice eventually it's like using a telescope to reveal a distant galaxy. It's the trick novelists employ. The writer, Henry James, famously said action reveals character. It's true for fiction and just as true in the stranger world of reality.

Imagine a moment when you have only a limited time to observe someone like at a gas station. From just a few actions you can extrapolate all sorts of predictions about their future behavior. You will be generalizing. You will sometimes be wrong. But more often that not, if you pay attention, you'll notice the way a person does one thing indicates the way they'll do the next thing.

Like... How a guy pumps gas will illustrate how he'll be in bed.

Consider his arrival. Does he pull up to the pump, slam on the brakes and make the car rock to a stop? Or does he ease up very slowly and gently apply the brakes to bring the car to a full and complete stop? Once he's out from behind the driver's seat, does the guy rush to pay, swiping his card with the speed of a hammer strike? Or is he the type to awkwardly fumble getting his card out of his wallet? Perhaps, he's a little bit geeky and bespectacled and he squints to read the tiny electronic numbers on the display, but you notice, he's gentle with the keypad buttons so the transaction goes slow but smoothly. And you know there's nothing wrong with slow and smooth.

Of course, there's the obvious question. How does he insert the nozzle? Is he rough with it, forcing it in with no regard to the car? Or is he awkward about it, scratching the car with the metal tip? Does it take him three clumsy attempts to get the darn thing in? Or does he casually slide it in? Obviously, not his first time pumping gas.

And let's say you have a little time on your hands, so you watch what he does while the gas pumps and he waits. Does he start grooming himself in public like an ape at the zoo? Or does he immediately get back in the car and start air drumming to some shitty band you don't like? Does he keep staring at the under-aged girl leaning against her shitbox Nissan with Wisconsin plates? Or does he stare at himself, admiring his reflection in the somewhat mirrored aluminum paneling of the gas pump? Maybe he notices you and flashes a small smile, since he caught you watching him. Oh, look he has a sense of humor.

When the gas is finally done pumping, how he finishes is just as important. Sometimes, it's more telling. Having gotten what he came for does he yank the nozzle out and quickly, almost automatically, slam it back into the pump and drive away? Or does he pull out too early and wind up shooting gas all down the side of the car? Or maybe he's careful to ease the gas nozzle back into the gas pump? Is he the sort who lets you pull out your car first so you can easily merge with the flow of traffic? Does he smile just before you drive away?

From a stolen moment at a gas station-you get a pretty good sense of a guy, and with a little imagination you can picture how he does other things. It works on anyone. And it works on you. Others can detect what you're like just by watching how you do what you do.

By the way, I hope you understood the car wasn't some sexist metaphor comparing a woman to a car. Nor did it imply a woman getting gassed-up by a bunch of different dudes. The car of this particular metaphor could've just as easily been a totally transgender SUV. It's not about the sexual attraction, or the car, it's about how a person reveals their way in everything they do.

An action, a single human moment is a symphony of movement and motivation. And if you want to understand other people, why waste your time listening to them talk when you can watch the ballet of their behavior dance before you. Ignore a person's words. Watch them. You'll find they'll gladly show you who they are. And this is just as true for you. You are your choices... and they become your way through the world.

* *

How To Find Love… (According To The Films Of Johnny Depp)

T housands of years ago, Chinese doctors discovered how acupuncture works by studying the war wounds of soldiers struck by arrows. With the right sort of eyes, you can learn all sorts of awesome lessons from the most unexpected places. Someday, if you look you just might find a diamond ring in the toilet. Now, let's be clear, I'm not implying Johnny Depp's filmography resembles a metaphorical toilet. Nor am I suggesting his acting is shitty. I'm not being coy. And I'm no fanboy. But I do think his work is an interesting place to pull advice on finding love. And most likely, you've seen his films. They're common coin of the realm. I guess we could use anything, from bird watching to the moon landing, as our example. But the first one seems sexist and the second one seems ridiculous. Johnny Depp films feel just right, kinda like Goldilocks' porridge. The dude is that rare sort of celebrity, a genuinely likable, seemingly fun and yet mysterious Hollywood icon. Men want to be him and women want to be with him. And his presumed integrity seems to guide his way through life. I'd argue there are a number of lessons we could learn from him and his work, but let's focus on what he might teach us about finding love.

Rather than bookmark another self-help website or listen to more advice from your idiot friends and opinionated family members, here's fresh advice on finding love.

BLOW

Drug dealers like George Jung, the hustler Johnny Depp played in Blow, are nothing if not optimistic. They see the risk they run and they think-*I can beat the system*. And until they become too greedy, they often do. This movie is a study in greed and bad decisions. The guy had a good thing going until he started messing around with cocaine and Penelope Cruz. But how can you blame him? I'd risk it all for Penelope Cruz, too. As Johnny's character shows us the downside of cocaine distribution, George Jung also illustrates a great truth of drug dealing that directly applies to finding love. Drug cartels operate in a shifting, ever-changing world. The route they used yesterday won't work next week. How they smuggled the last shipment won't work on the next shipment. Tomorrow always requires new approaches. If you're struggling to find love, you probably go to the same places and hang out with the same people. It may be time you try some new shit. Go to new restaurants and coffeehouses. Go to neighborhoods where you don't know anyone. Learn about new artists and go see their work at a gallery opening. Take a class. Join a club. Get your ass out there where new people can appreciate you. But do this stuff for you! Don't do it to meet new people. The point is to refresh you. Newness helps you see the world differently. It keeps you interested and shining with enthusiasm. ... And stay away from cocaine, kids.

PUBLIC ENEMIES

I love a good '30s gangster/bank robber movie. And this one didn't disappoint. There were the men-hanging-off-cars shooting Tommy-guns scenes. There were the prison breaks and bank robberies. There were all those great haircuts and suits and '30s dresses. There were the quiet moments hiding out in a farmhouse in the middle of nowhere. I love all that shit. Johnny Depp seems to as well. He looked comfortable living in those imaginary circumstances. The great thing about crime films is how they show our values in reverse like a photographic negative. More than say a film about a small town and how everyone depends on everyone-when you show a bunch of gangsters on the lam, you learn all you need to know about trust between partners and how self-interest balances against what's best for the group. Gangsters depend on their shared culture. They need to know the difference between a grunt and a head nod, a silent look and a thousand-yard stare. They have to be able to speak and understand body language if they plan on trusting anyone. When you're dating, it's best when you two "get" each other without a lot of extra words. However, don't be small-minded about this. It doesn't mean don't date someone from a different race, culture or creed. Opposites attract and can make love exciting. So... yes, you can date a Jewish girl even if you're uncircumcised. But it helps a ton if you both love '90s hip-hop. That way you speak the same language and you already share a similar culture.

FEAR & LOATHING IN LAS VEGAS

They went to Las Vegas to find the American Dream, instead they found the high-water mark where the cultural wave broke and the generational tide receded. It's an enormous understanding to reach, and in order to do so, Dr. Gonzo and Raoul Duke, the characters Johnny Depp and Benicio del Toro play in the movie, needed to be outsized, to be ridiculous, to be pariahs. And despite all the drugs they do, all the destruction they leave in their wake and the madness they spread, they did find what they were looking for-the death of the American Dream. The movie captures that sad hinge of American history in all its psychedelic strangeness. And sometimes your love life might feel like a crazy bad acid trip, or worse, a depraved ether binge. But you gotta remember you'll find exactly what you're looking for as long as you expect things will get weird before you find it. Unfortunately, often you'll have to go out with all those mouth-breathers and empty-headed clones, but they help you appreciate it when you find the one you want. If your friends or flat-mates see that you're struggling in the dating scene, they may tell you "have fun," "be yourself" and "be in the moment." Not bad advice. But if it confuses you... here's the secret of how to "be in the moment?" One word... **Curiosity.** Talk to the guy with the orangutan in the casino bar. He may be the key. Be as curious as Hunter S. Thompson.

On your next date, don't focus on you or talk a lot about you. Don't obsess about how you're coming across. Instead, pay attention to your date. Find something about them that intrigues you. When you're genuinely curious, the conversation will flow naturally. If you still struggle to find something about them that interests you then... boom! They're a waste of your time. That's how to go gonzo on the dating scene.

ED WOOD

This is probably one of his movies you might have missed. It was about a B-movie filmmaker, the titular, Ed Wood. If you haven't seen the film, it's worth watching just to see Johnny Depp in a skirt and angora sweater as he barks orders on a film set. But you'll also see, the key to Ed Wood's character isn't his cross-dressing, it's the fact he's charismatically persistent. The guy refuses to give up. It takes a shit-ton of effort to make a movie happen. You've read how many names scroll past in the end credits. To keep that creative juggernaut moving forward a film needs at least one person who keeps pushing despite all the million challenges and crises that threaten collapse of an independent production. *Ed Wood* is a study in the necessity of delusional optimism. When rationally it feels like you'll never find love and you have 1,001 reasons why you know that's sadly true, your love life is the B-movie you have to make no matter how many forces seem to align against you. When he felt particularly stressed out, Ed Wood, liked to slip into something a little more comfortable, like the aforementioned pencil skirt and angora sweater. They helped him cope. The angora helped him keep going. Whatever it takes, as long as you keep going.

PIRATES OF THE CARIBBEAN

Obviously, pirates like Captain Jack Sparrow don't generally give a fuck about breaking the laws of the land or the sea. Yet, you will notice everyone's favorite fictional pirate does have his own "rules." There's also "The Code" amongst all pirates, but as is often pointed out, "It's really more like guidelines." However, the personal code of Captain Jack does guide him. It makes him somewhat paradoxical. He tells the truth yet he will happily betray people. He has no love for partnerships but he will begrudgingly protect his partners and risk his life to save theirs. I'm not saying he's any paragon of virtue but you know what to expect when you strike a bargain with Capt. Jack Sparrow. Whenever you start a new relationship, you become "partners-in-crime." Which means you must establish "The Code" of your new partnership. You can't just assume you share the same rules or that your partner knows what your rules are. If you hate when he responds to your phone-call with a text message, you need to let him know, rather than assume he knows "that shit's rude." Maybe it just means he's busy.

CHOCOLAT

Gypsies on boats, chocolate that overpowers small minds and petty bureaucracies, beautiful French women, and Johnny Depp playing guitar... How can anyone not like this movie? It's got something for everyone. And it's a fun throwback look at how traditions and customs shackle us and restrain us from really fully living and loving. And you'll notice Johnny Depp's gypsy guitarist gets it. He expects life's little troubles but they don't ruin his day. He knows he and his people are outsiders. He doesn't expect to be welcomed or appreciated. But he does demand that folks respect him and those like him. Others learn how to treat you based on... how you treat yourself... as well as how you treat them. Fear is terribly unsexy. It dooms relationships. Love and loyalty require mutual respect. Offer your new partner respect for her time, for his friends, for her high-powered job, for his silly hobbies. Ignore your fears and respect their choices. The minute you stop respecting your partner, it's time to leave. And if they don't respect you, it's time for them to go. Better to kill the relationship and start over. And sometimes you have to go, even when you don't want to. Trust me... and Juliette Binoche, it's for the best.

DONNIE BRASCO

Here's an exceedingly simple yet difficult lesson from a Johnny Depp film. Again, it comes from a crime film. This time he played an undercover cop who infiltrated the mob and was lying to expose the truth. That's the not the takeaway lesson. I'm not arguing that you start playing mind games. That's for teenagers and underdeveloped adults. After a few years of being an actual-factual adult, you'll see all the ways love can ruin a person, and often in response we grow hesitant or gun-shy, possibly even cynical. What Donnie Brasco shows us is the need to take bigger risks. Push your limits. The only way to do something wildly impossible and impractical, both of which certainly describe love, you must be willing to risk it all. Life, limb, and liberty.

Embrace the danger of embarrassment. No one's going to shoot you in the face or dump you in the East river, but on the road to love you will risk terribly awkward moments. Those happen anyway. So act tough even when you feel like everyone can see the truth that you're scared shitless. The next time you overhear a guy talking and he sounds cool, ask out the cute stranger, even if you're sure he'll say "no." If you have a crush on the girl you often see when you're at your local laundry, next time ask her out. Like an undercover cop you gotta have the eggs to take on big risks. If you really want it, you gotta have the balls to go after what you want.

CHARLIE AND THE CHOCOLATE FACTORY

I prefer the first film. To me Gene Wilder *IS* Willie Wonka. But I have total respect for what Tim Burton and Johnny Depp tried to do. It was sure fun to look at. And they definitely captured the legend of Willie Wonka and understood how one man's myth can change the world. That's what you need, an interesting myth about you.

Since most folks today ignore advertising, these days we mostly trust word-of-mouth recommendations. Well, this includes you. If people like to tell stories about you, perhaps someone-you-know has friends and workmates who keep hearing about you. Maybe one of them will want to meet you. The key to a "good myth" is... don't hype yourself. Tell funny stories. If you're genuine you'll attract people who appreciate you the way you are. We all distrust a salesman. Selectively be self-revealing and tell stories about the funny shit that you do or that happens to you. Share your "myth." And let others do your advertising.

DON JUAN DEMARCO

"When I say that all my women are dazzling beauties, they object. The nose of this one is too large; the-the hips of another, they are too wide; perhaps the breasts of a third, they are too small. But I see these women for how they truly are... glorious, radiant, spectacular, and perfect, because, I am not limited by my eyesight. Women react to me the way that they do, Don Octavio, because they sense that I search out the beauty that dwells within until it overwhelms everything else."

-Don Juan DeMarco

It was kinda cheesy, but I totally enjoyed this film, not just because Brando and Johnny Depp were acting together, that helped, but mostly because how it captured the delusions of love, and how it showed us romance is a form of madness. The best possible madness you'll ever know. If Johnny Depp's character, Don Juan de Marco, is crazy, he will tell you he is only crazy... for women. This should be your attitude about love. You don't need someone in your life. You desire someone special in your life. You seek pleasure and deep connection. Which means, you must be very discerning. You may need to wait until you find someone who is undeniably attractive. Someone who drives you mad with desire. And if you want love that's not some teen fantasy, you must also remember your romantic partner affects everything. To balance the delusions of love, one must also find a person who fits your life, who compliments you and the way you are. It can't all be intoxicating madness. That's a different film. That's *Sid & Nancy*.

In order to see how you and your beloved fit, travel together. See what your new boyfriend is like when he's jet-lagged. If you get sick, ask your new girlfriend to pick something up at the store. Go camping and see how they handle the world without their usual comforts. Take her to an ethnic neighborhood and watch how she treats the waitress. On a first date, ask him to tell you a funny story from when he was a teenager. Life is way too stressful to be with someone who doesn't make you laugh. Don't get a partner just to cure your boredom or as a status symbol. You want someone who makes you braver, makes you better and drives you crazy with desire. A difficult mix to find, but as Johnny Depp's films will show you it helps if you're a little bit delusional. Romance is a beautiful madness and love is irrational, yet they're worth every obstacle you must overcome.

* *

Why Women's Biological Clocks
Scare The Shit Out Of Men

S ome guy once told me to watch out because all women change when they turn twenty-five. Personally, I prefer not to generalize people, unless the generalization is terribly obvious like: *all people tend to die when they eat cyanide.* That's actually useful and true. The rest of the time, whenever we generalize it promotes dangerously lazy thinking and we rely on arbitrary standards to group people together, things like race, class, politics, sexual persuasion and gender. Not all black people are good dancers. Not all gay people dress well. Not all Republicans are selfish assholes. And not all women change when they turn twenty-five.

But damned, if I wasn't surprised to see a high percentage of the women I know turn twenty-five and suddenly their priorities switched. Suddenly, these otherwise independent-minded women, ones who were former punk rockers, footloose world-tripping travelers, and highly focused ladder-climbing career women, begin to often and openly discuss marriage, babies and husbands. It was like overnight, the Ugly Truth Fairy visited them and instead of teeth, she took their carefree ways and instead of cash she left under their pillow a biological clock to drive them insane. I guess I'd say most of the girls I knew suddenly grew up and became women.

This isn't a new phenomenon. This isn't some millennial issue. This is some old world pressure. The cynical filmmaker, Billy Wilder, once made a joke about this social phenomenon in his film, *Some Like It Hot*. While on a train to Florida, Marilyn Monroe's nightclub singer character, Sugar, reflects on her life.

Sugar says, *"I'm twenty-five years old. That's a quarter of century. Makes a girl think."*

The character played by Tony Curtis, Josephine, asks her, *"About what?"*

Sugar answers, *"You know-like a husband."*

That was sixty years ago. We should remember this was dialog scripted by two middle-aged men writing for laughs. But the understood pressure of being a twenty five-year old girl was common enough the audience got the joke. Feminists fought for centuries to give women a sense of freedom from such antiquated baby-making responsibilities and assumptions that getting wifed-up was their biggest goal in life. However, Marilyn's dialog could fit in any rom-com from today and no woman would bat an eyelash or call it anachronistic. Today's young women still seem to see turning twenty-five as the same dreaded dividing line.

Any person who's spent some time around a twenty five-year old man will tell you how young men experience little to none of this time pressure, internal or external. A twenty five-year old man is doing damn well in most people's eyes if he has a clean bathroom and some social plans past this weekend. He isn't expected to have plans for anything as meaningful as babies, a family and a home for them to enjoy. It seems only young women suffer from the tick-tock of the imagined biological clock.

It doesn't matter whether it's an internal sense of her biological clock or if it's external social pressure. The effect is the same. And most times, it's a combination of both internal fears and external pressures from family, friends and society. Most young Western women feel this squeeze. They each react differently, but the pressure seems shared. And consequently, this gender-based time-based divide bedevils and stresses young relationships between men and women, and unfairly so. It leaves young women feeling as if they must drag the men in their lives into maturity. And the young men wonder why women constantly demand they act in ways that don't yet feel natural to them since the men don't use the same life clock.

Everyone knows girls mature faster than boys. It's as obvious as the squeak in a teen boy's voice, and easily recognizable from the height differences in junior high when girls often tower over their boy classmates. By the time, we're adults it seems although the height gap gets corrected the "time gap" never truly disappears. Women are seemingly always one step ahead of men in terms of maturation.

Some evolutionary biologists suggest women's menstruation is responsible for our shared notions of time. The fact that women could regularly track cycles of their body as reliably as the phases of the moon gave them a sense of anticipation of life cycles. While men used a much slower "clock" based on the longer seasonal cycles of hunting and farming to make sense of the changes of life from one day to the next.

For millennia, humans relied on sundials, hourglasses and candle-clocks to keep track of the passing of the hours of the day. The mechanical clock as we would recognize it, was invented in 1094 C.E. by the Chinese monk, Su Sung. In medieval times, European clergy needed to ensure they could wake up at the same time every day to complete their morning prayers. They relied on mechanical clocks to keep reliable time as they slept. And their use of mechanical clocks helped spread the standardized time until gradually it was used the world over. Men may have given us the clock and our modern sense of mechanical time, but a woman's internal clock is still far more important to society than the tick-tick-ticking of any man's clock. The reason is simple. Her biological clock has a finite window. One day it will stop.

Rather than a clock, we really ought to consider it more of a countdown. And seen as such, women aren't motivated by time as much as they're motivated by opportunity. They're like athletes who know their bones, joints and muscles won't always allow them to perform at their peak level and thus, they really need to do their thing while they can. Most men like sports metaphors. A man understands the world of sports even if he never played anything other than soccer video games.

Perhaps, rather than speaking of a woman's biological clock, we should describe it as woman has "peak years" of her baby-making career. Maybe if we speak of her desire to bring home a few "championships," men would stop feeling the pressure, and they'd no longer see it as some sort of negative consequence for them. Instead, men would view their relationship with the woman in their life as something of a team sport, one wherein they'd want to do everything they can to help bring home some "trophies. "

This may all sound kinda silly to you. But you have to understand that to a twenty-five year old man, presumably a few years out of college, or a few years into his career as a blue-collar guy not quite able to start his own company but perhaps finally earning a steady and meaty paycheck, taking on the responsibilities of a baby and family seems daunting. It seems like, for lack of a better metaphor, a life sentence. And thus, there's a certain reluctance to grow-up. He sees it as the end of his freedom. Sure, he may love his girlfriend, he may want to spend his foreseeable future with her, but the sense of urgency and the related demands placed on him feel arbitrary and forced.

This is why many young dudes give mixed messages. And this confusion makes the woman in his life doubt his sincerity and value as a partner. To her family and friends his hesitation appears to be concrete evidence of the fact he's not the right guy for her. And perhaps due to these doubts and outside influences an otherwise healthy partnership buckles under the weight of expectations.

Thinking back to a few generations ago, when a guy got a girl pregnant, it meant he knew he had to do the "right thing" and marry her. If he was reluctant, outside pressure was offered in the form of a shotgun. Those days are gone. When was the last time you were invited to a shotgun wedding? The thing is, with so many forms of birth control on the market, attitudes about babies shifted. Sex became far more about pleasure and seduction. I refuse to entertain any moral arguments about the impact of this shift because honestly, I don't care. There are plenty of people on the planet and I don't feel anyone should feel any pressure to add to the numbers. However, if you want to have a baby, which many young people still do, the timing of that decision is paramount.

Women are finding growing opportunities for careers and decisions that were not available to them decades ago. But rather than shift their focus from being mothers to being career-minded young women, they've enlarged their expectations for themselves. And now today we hear a great deal about the struggles for a woman to have it all- a thriving career, a happy marriage, a growing family, a beautiful and well-kept home, a healthy and sexy body, and also enjoy the occasional exciting vacation and adventures outside of work. That's a really full plate. Men don't seem to have such a full appetite. Generally speaking.

If this "have-it-all" plan (for a heternormative life) is attainable, it requires at the foundation, a strong partnership with a man of her choosing. And one aspect of a strong partnership is the need to redefine what that is and what it looks like. More and more men are finding it works well for them and their family if they're the stay-at-home partner/dad. Being a stay-at-home man is a growing trend. But it's not quite something to be proud of at your ten-year high school reunion.

We ought to consider the expanded opportunities for women in the boardroom as equivalent to expanded opportunities for men in the family room. A readjustment of our values of what it means to be a woman and what it means to be a man will guarantee greater happiness for both in the bedroom.

If young men can remember women aren't pushing them to "grow up" faster, instead they're looking for strong teammates to help them bring home a few "championships" while they're in their peak years of their baby-making careers, men will better relate and become eager teamplayers. And if women, start considering a man who's willing to be a stay-at-home partner as a sexy and desirable man, then other men would stop sneering and joking and demeaning the guys who run households. Because trust me, men take their cues from women. Part of the reason men respect alpha-males is because women desire alpha-males. But as women become alphas, a seismic shift is underway, one that requires women to expand their sense of what's sexy and what a good partner looks like. There are not enough alpha men for all the new alpha women. And if these high-achieving women have any hope for life-long happiness they need to consider the idea that behind any successful woman there could be a man.

Luckily, from studies of female sexuality, we're learning that women are just as turned-on by images of a hot young shirtless man as they are by seeing a man burping his baby at a ballgame. Female sexuality seems to be far more motivated by intimacy than mere appearances and if this is the case, with social pressures changing perhaps female sexuality will soon find stay-at-home-dads sexy. And if this happens, biological clocks will become less of a punchline, be less a source of stress, and more like a team-building exercise. Remember we're all on the same side and just like the Quiet Game... everyone wants to win.

* *

In Relationships: Are You The Lover or the Beloved?

W henever a friend has trouble in their relationship, I always ask the same question.

"Are you the bird... or are you the hand?"

Some friends think the question suggests one of them in the relationship loves the other more. That's not true. Their love is equal. It's just expressed totally differently. It's like how the word for love isn't pronounced the same by a German as a Korean. But it's definitely the same feeling.

The idea is childishly simple. Which is why I know it's true. Einstein said if a complex idea can be explained in simple terms it means one understands it. I've thought a lot about it and this analogy works for all love relationships.

"The bird and the hand" is pretty much the $E=mc^2$ of love.

Here it is. In relationships, there are two roles: the lover and the beloved. You've seen this dynamic at play in your relationships, as well as your friends and family. It's a variation on "opposites attract." And it's as natural as magnetism.

You may not believe me. So... let's use some celebrities we all know and test this "bird and the hand" dynamic.

Ozzie and Sharon Osbourne. They've been together for ages and clearly they love each other. Ozzie is the bird and Sharon is the hand. Ozzie needs to be free to fly, to go off and be as weird as he is. And Sharon needs to nurture Ozzie. She understands his nature and knows he will always return to her. If Sharon tried to keep him tight to her, Ozzie would fly away for good. And if Sharon thought Ozzie wasn't going to return, she'd go and find a new bird to love. She knows Ozzie will come back so she leaves her hand open. Ozzie's certain Sharon cares for him and won't smother him with her love, so he happily returns.

This dynamic requires trust and confidence. This is where most folks run into trouble. A lack of trust and confidence dooms relationships more often than the word "Facebook" shows up in divorce filings. Birds need to be confident the hand will hold them, yet will also let them go. And the hand must trust the bird loves them even when it flies away.

Think of Jessica Biel and Justin Timberlake. Jessica's a total hand. She wants to hold Justin, who's about as flighty as they come. She's learned to trust him and keep her hand open. He's confident she'll be warm when he returns, yet will let him go again. They finally got married when she understood a caged bird doesn't sing as pretty.

Let's be clear, it's not always a woman who's the nurturer. Sometimes, it's the dude. Jay-Z is a hand and Beyonce is the bird. It's the same for Brangelina. Brad Pitt is a total hand. Angelina Jolie is his beloved bird.

She wants what she wants and he goes along with it. Brad's happy to have her in his life. He was content to build "green" houses in New Orleans, while she flew around the world on UN Missions. This dynamic works for them.

However, when Brad Pitt was married to Jennifer Aniston, he tried to be the bird. And she was the hand that held him. That didn't work so well. They were actually both hands and two hands don't make a fun couple. Brad wandered away because... he desired to hold a bird, not to hold hands.

When two hands grip each other, their tight squeeze lacks surprise. It grows boring and airless. So... when a new bird caught Brad's eye, he couldn't deny his stifling boredom. Down deep he knew he's a hand and he wanted to hold a bird. It's the only way for him to be happy. It's his nature.

Brad and Angelina also prove both the hand and bird are equally sexy. Don't get hung up on the imagery of the metaphor. It's just an analogy.

Moving from one relationship to the next, your role may switch. And sometimes, in a relationship, you might take turns being the bird or the hand. This is a delicate dance and takes a very dedicated effort. If the timing is ever off, or you aren't ready to switch roles, or you try to convince yourself you're ready to switch when you really aren't... everything will fall apart like a trailer park in a tornado.

It's what happened to Johnny Depp and Vanessa Paradis. They were a daring and fun couple, so loving and free, yet anchored in the fluid rhythms of their family. They took turns being the bird and the hand... but eventually, they were tested by the twister of time and their relationship was flattened. It's a difficult dance to keep forever in rhythm... especially when storms begin to blow.

So... what happens when two free-spirited birds get together? Usually, they don't spend enough time together or communicate well and soon all the freedom between them turns the relationship sad and ugly, like bird shit on a wedding dress.

Think of Kanye West and Kim Kardashian. They're both birds. And yes, I know... betting on a Kim Kardashian relationship ending is kinda like betting on the sun rising. Way too easy. My advice to Kanye is, now that he's also a father, he better always be the hand if he wants his relationship with Kim to work out. Some folks say Kim isn't really the bird... they say she's actually *the beard.* So, let's just keep moving.

A bird is happy to sing its song and be appreciated, to have a warm place to land and occasionally be held. While, a hand is happy to stroke soft feathers and listen to the song, to nurture the bird whenever it occasionally returns. The key word here isn't *happy*... but "occasionally." Birds need occasional freedom and hands need occasional surprise.

Fear, paranoia and jealousy, will make a hand crush a bird in its grip, or make the bird fly away to save itself. While neglect and mistrust will make a hand feel like the bird will never return, and eventually it finds a new bird, one it can hold.

The key to happiness in your relationship is to know who's the bird and who's the hand. Then make sure you don't expect a hand to fly or a bird to hold you.

* *

One Really Big Bed: On Being In A Three-Person Relationship

A friend of mine has two boyfriends and they all live together in a house they bought. I call them The Funboys. It's just the most fitting name ever. They travel together. They cook together. They garden together. They laugh together. They love together. And they sleep together in a giant king-size bed.

More than what they do in the bedroom, I've always been curious about how three grown men all share one bed. I constantly ask: Do you use the same alarm clock? Who sleeps in the middle-do you take turns? Do you cuddle and spoon together three in a row? Seems like it'd be awesome in the winter but what about the summertime? ...Sounds kinda sweaty.

Luckily, because I've known them for years, I don't sound like I'm asking lesbians how they have sex. Instead, I'm more like some annoyingly curious kid who just really wants to know. And I do. I really want to know how they make it all work. Not just the emotional parts but also the logistics of three men in a bed. It turns out it's the same answer. When you love each other, you figure out the small things like who sleeps next to the alarm clock the same way you figure out the big questions. You consider what works for the other(s) and what works for you. Sometimes you compromise. Sometimes you triage and take care of what matters most. There are no one-size-fits-all answers to questions of relationships. Love is a constant negotiation.

If you were wondering, they each have a favorite spot in bed but sometimes it changes from night to night based on who needs to be up earliest and who feels like cuddling. And the alarm clock is only for one of them since the other two set their own work schedules. That way there's no fight over the snooze bar.

Naturalists recognize some plants grow better together. They call it companion planting. Some tribes of American Indians used the "Three Sisters" system of growing corn, squash and beans together on the same plot of land. The harvest provided a balanced diet and grown together the plants were an effective farming strategy. Corn grows tall and offers a structure for climbing beans to cling to. The beans and corn don't compete for nutrients since beans provide their own nitrogen. The squash grows as ground cover and shades the weeds that might compete with the beans and corn. Each has a role to play. Nature may like pairs but it's not always limited to them. It seems Nature prefers dynamic responsive relationships more than number sets.

Other than death, nothing in life seems to be as scary and confusing, as troublesome and endlessly debated, as how we choose to love one another. Gay marriage is a ridiculous issue. The fact anyone gets a say about who you love, how you love, to whom you pledge your life and loyalty is insufferably ignorant. The fact that interracial marriage is still an issue for anyone is embarrassing. The idea adults who choose to love each other are ever limited by other people is irretrievably stupid.

The major religions and philosophies agree love is our highest pursuit. Yet, we often define love with childish rules like it's a game. We outline areas where a person is out-of-bounds. Far as I can tell love is boundless. As long as the adults involved aren't hurting anyone and aren't being hurt, no outsider should stand in their way.

My three friends who all live and love together have taught me more about love than my divorced parents did. Like the gardens they grow in their front and backyards, the Funboys tend to their love. And they let love take its own natural shape. I like that. It's reassuring. I've had girlfriends who had specific expectations of what love looked like based on images they collected from television, movies, advertisements, friends' stories, magazine articles, blog posts, pretty much everywhere but from conversations between us. Living in an imitation of others' happiness never works for me. It'd be like moving into a model home, only to discover the books are all cardboard fronts and the flowers are cloth and plastic. I have to live in a way that makes sense to me. And I don't believe there is any one natural way to love. Just like there's no one way to eat an Oreo.

I once tried dating a married woman. It wasn't like it sounds. She and her husband were polyamorists. We all lived in Berkeley where such attitudes seem almost commonplace. When she and I first started dating I had to visit the restaurant she and her husband owned so I could meet him and get his blessing. After what was one of the more uncomfortable dinners of my life, he decided I was a good guy and he gave his blessing for me to date his wife. If you think getting a blessing from a girl's family is difficult imagine a woman's husband. It all seemed kinda sexist to me until she explained she gave her blessing to his girlfriends, too. It was part of their "rules."

I wish I could say everything went smoothly but it didn't. It felt weird to me. I pass no judgment on polyamorists. I defend their right to love whomever and however they choose. The reason it felt weird was there were always others in our relationship, people I couldn't communicate with. For instance, on one of our dates, she casually mentioned her three small children were staying with a babysitter. Her husband was out with his side-girlfriend. She was out with me. And the kids were home with a sitter. I asked how long she and her husband had been side-dating.

The whole arrangement was his idea. He had gone through a few girlfriends, but I was the first guy she'd chosen to date. They were married at eighteen because she got pregnant. They'd just graduated from high school when she found out. They had two more kids. Opened a successful restaurant. And made a go of it as full-fledged adults.

I asked why she was so insistent we go out that night. I'd assumed her husband was home with their kids. The timing of my curiosity wasn't the best. We'd been making out in her car. We were both topless when I asked. Rather than answer, she started crying. She said her husband had subtly pushed her to take up a side-lover to "spice things up." I stopped asking questions and just held her. I had all the answers I needed.

I knew it was time we stopped seeing each other but I didn't say anything that night. On our next date, I told her. Again, she cried. She thought I was rejecting her, which might've brought up the same feelings as her husband's subtler rejection. I don't know. I told her I was competing with her children for her attention and it didn't feel good. She said she understood.

Days later she showed up at my house, looking to share some expensive bottle of wine from her restaurant and wanting to figure out how we could continue seeing each other. I told her about my friends who share one happy bed. And how I learned love takes its own shape. There's no limit to how many loves and lovers a person can have. Some folks have amazing capacities for love. I believe in asexuality, monogamy, polyamory and May-December love affairs. There are no requirements one should place on love other than... honesty and commitment.

I also said, from my time with her, I learned that the more people who enter into a relationship, the more important honesty becomes. Not truth-that's a matter of fact versus fiction. I mean honesty-the ability to share your opinions in an open and forthright way. The Funboys make love work because they're open and honest with each other. The same as how it works within any relationship. They know it's imperative each person feel safe to speak up when they feel hurt, scared, neglected or left out of the decision-making process. They all commit to each other.

Without honesty, lust and desire can trick you and pretend to be love. Attachment will masquerade as commitment. My married girlfriend wasn't being honest with herself. She was scared. She was hurt. She was acting like the teenage girl and young twenty-something women she never got to be. She accused me of being a traditionalist, kinda like she was calling me a racist or a sexist, some equally horrible label based on prejudice. Sometimes people seem to think they can shame you into doing what they want. It doesn't usually work on me because I have to live with whatever I do.

I reiterated my simple understanding of love, "As long as you aren't hurting anyone... and you aren't being hurt... then you can do whatever you want."

The sad part was she knew she was hurting her kids. She knew she was hurting herself. She knew there was no way to deny it. But she still wanted to ignore all that pain because sometimes being an adult is far more difficult than anyone prepares you for. And she just wanted to feel loved and adored and sexy and desired.

Much like Mondrian's increasingly abstract paintings of a tree, which began as imaginative renderings of a tree's shape, but soon progressed to the point all one saw were lines and boundaries suggesting the shape of something once common and familiar, our adult love story no longer had much recognizable love in it. I told her we'd reached my boundary, even if she wanted to go on. She said a few more things about how I was a closet conservative. Normally, I would've laughed. Calling me a closet conservative is like calling Liberace a closeted straight man. But she wasn't really talking to me, so I listened as she spit her angry hot words. It was the last time we spoke.

From The Funboys I've learned well and true how to love my partner and myself, and if need be, more than one person in a healthy, supportive way. From the polyamorists I learned the risks of loving more than one person, especially if you're the third or fourth person in the bed. And from life, and all its strangeness, I've learned I don't want to be in a relationship with more than one person. That's just me. I still feel there is no one-size-fits-all rule for relationships. But there are two requirements for love... honesty and commitment.

* *

An Orgasm-A-Day... For A Better Tomorrow!

W e live in a society that's always selling sex. Pushing it at you in strange places like in advertisements for car insurance. If you watch sports, you know, every other ad seems to be for pecker pills, drugs with silly names that'll make your dick stiff. And for women it seems every magazine cover promises to teach you the secrets of how to make your man happier in the bedroom... or how and why you single women should be friendly with your vibrator. Advertisers and editors and sales-force teams all seem to love sex more than the Marquis de Sade.

The thing is... they're not wrong. Sex is awesome. It's so powerful it'll make you buy shit you don't need. That's why they're using it against you. Using it to scare you. They want you to believe you're doing it all wrong, you're not doing it enough, everyone's doing it but you. They're fucking with you when they sell sex.

Consequently, we remain strangely uncomfortable with sex. It's all over pop culture, yet we have weird attitudes about it. Girlfriends chat about it. Dudes brag about it. But we never really talk about it in any substantive way. And Americans are less mature about sex than most every other country in the world. We're afraid of it. And I think the reason is, we love sex, but we're intimidated by orgasms.

Men in America only recently learned how to find a clitoris or the G-spot. Even in the '90s most American men weren't yet on a first-name basis with the clitoris. They don't like to say the word in mixed company. It sounds like a challenge. And from what I hear, foreplay is something straight men perform begrudgingly and usually without much imagination. Which makes me curious about how much foreplay is expected in gay male sex.

Sadly, American women are plagued with psychological barriers to enjoying orgasms. Numerous studies show that around 15% of women have never experienced an orgasm and nearly 50% experience infrequent orgasms. Doctors will point out how 99% of women are physically capable of orgasms but they become psychologically incapable. Women often experience anxiety about sex, especially receiving oral sex. It seems like most women have self-conscious fears about the moist and fragrant world beneath their beltline.

For the record, any guy who gets to put his face in your special space... he's lucky! If some dude makes you feel bad about your vagina then he's an asshole. Or he's immature and intimidated by anything with any sense of mystery and earthiness. So get rid of him and find someone who will eat you out like you have a five-star restaurant between your thighs.

The real question is: *Why are we all so sexually uncomfortable-why do we act like adolescents who want sex but are equally afraid of it?*

You can't entirely blame your parents because I doubt they talked with you much about sex. And they probably don't know much either. The one to blame has to be our culture in general. If it's our shared culture that makes us so hung-up on sex... then we need to change our culture.

I have a simple plan. We focus on orgasms and we'll work our way out from there.

We need to talk about what we like. What we don't like. What we know. Ask questions about what we don't know. We don't need to be "grossed out" by any aspect of sex. When I've told women I was sleeping with that I'm not afraid of period blood and we could still have sex, and that I'd just change the sheets and we could shower together afterwards, the women looked at me with the same shock they might experience if I said I like to eat dogshit dipped in chocolate sauce. I always thought-*What's the big deal?*

With my last girlfriend, I came up with a cute euphemism so I didn't have to say the words blood or period, because they made her feel "icky." So I said I didn't care about getting "rusty." I knew she wanted to have sex but she didn't want me to be "all grossed-out." Ha! I had to explain, I'd cut myself before. I knew what blood looked like. I knew she had some in her body, too. And I desired her. I wanted to have sex. To me the period blood was no different than saliva or sweat or earwax. It's a bodily fluid. Big deal. Eventually, she relaxed. And we often had our best sex when we got "rusty" because she was on her moon.

So... let's talk frankly a moment about orgasms. We all have them. We all like them. Even people without genitals can experience them. Dead bodies can have them if you tap the right nerve. Babies in utero have been seen masturbating, or doing what clearly appears to be masturbation. We're hardwired for orgasms. If you're curious for some solid science on orgasms, check out Mary Roach's TED talk "10 Things You Didn't Know About Orgasms." It's pretty funny.

Modern science is finding orgasms are great for our health. They make us look ten years younger, feel better physically and psychologically, they stabilize our hormones, they make our hair and skin look healthy, they relieve tension and help you lose weight... the list goes on and on.

So... I recommend at least an orgasm-a-day. More if you have more time.

I'm sure some of you are thinking I don't like societal pressure to have sex. And I agree. Don't let anyone make you feel bad. I'm advocating you feel good... so if you prefer, masturbate. Even when you have no partner, make a little time for an orgasm.

Pleasuring yourself is a good habit because it subtly tells you you're worth it. And you exercise your creativity and imagination. You're taking some time for you. It's like yoga you don't pay for or have to travel anywhere to do it. Not that I'm saying give up yoga for orgasms. Just add an orgasm to your routine. And apparently for women, there's something called "yogasms." Look into it. Something about Kegel exercises and Downward Dog.

As for you asexual people who may not like my full-throated song of appreciation for all things orgasmic, I don't want to make you feel bad or excluded. I understand you don't feel sexual stimulation plays an important part in your life. And I get where you're coming from… well, kinda. I've read a bunch of your online forums to understand your worldview. As you can probably tell sex and orgasms are pretty important to me and have been for as long as I can remember.

A little background… when I was six and went to an afterschool program, I used to pretend I was injured. Almost daily. And I did it because one of the women who watched us had enormous breasts. I loved to press my head against her chest, and the truth is, I'd cop a feel. I knew that she'd never suspect a six-year old of having sexual thoughts and my cute innocent face could hide my interest in her breasts. I knew if I squeezed her boobs, to her, it was harmless because I was a kid. I know… it's embarrassing. A six-year old cuddle-molesting a grown woman. It's so backwards I don't even know what to think.

My point is, for those of you who are asexual, I totally don't get how you live that way. But I respect you and where you're coming from. And I would never recommend you do something you don't want to or don't feel comfortable doing, so if you want to live without a daily orgasm... I get it. And that's the last we'll speak of it.

For the rest of you, do yourself a favor and make sure you get off at least once a day. Trust me, it's good for you. If you need a little help, or perhaps some inspiration, check out-beautifulagony.com

It's a website entirely dedicated to the faces of orgasms. It's guys and girls. It's totally tasteful. No nudity. Just the face of a person as they masturbate or are pleasured into reaching an orgasm. It's... pretty awesome.

An orgasm-a-day!

...That's all I ask. You're doing it for you... and for me... and for our whole society.

If we start by making sure we each have an orgasm-a-day, we subtly tell ourselves we have value. We deserve it. We don't need to buy anything to make ourselves feel good and worthwhile. We just pleasure ourselves. And then, if we value and pleasure ourselves, maybe over time we can shift our valuing-and-pleasuring to others. And that'll lead to better sex. And then from better sex, we can enjoy better relationships and communication. And with better communication we can talk more openly and frankly about the world we share. And by doing that we can value our world, and seek pleasure in our world, and make sure others do the same. You see where I'm going with this.

One by one, your orgasms will help build a better future. So do it for you... for me... for all of us. Now go get yourself an orgasm!

* *

How Do You Forgive Someone Who Just Ruined Your Future?

W hen you wake up to a phone call from your best friend and business partner, and he tells you fire marshals from three different counties are waiting for you at the hilltop construction site of a million dollar dream-house and they have some questions they'd like to ask you... you don't have to wonder... it's gonna be a shitty day. No doubt about it. It's never awesome when fire marshals have questions and you're the one with the answers.

I said, "...Fire marshals, huh? Sure. I'll head out there right now. Was there a —"

My friend said, "Guess it's pretty bad. Don't know the details, but hurry up because they're waiting for you."

I should've said, "Okay... I'm headed to Mexico, but you tell them I said Reno."

I didn't say that because my life's not an outlaw country song from the Seventies. And I needed to go because my friend had just arrived home from a vacation and was still at the airport when the firemen called him. Then he called me. So off I went to answer the fire marshals' questions. While I drove, I asked myself the same question over and over again:

How do you forgive someone who ruined your future?

I wanted to know... because I was pretty sure I'd just ruined my best friend's future.

Somehow, I'd crossed a dividing line in my life. When I went to sleep, it was the time before the fire... and when I woke up it was the time after the fire.

My best friend and I grew up in a small college town. In the summer, we worked together painting rental houses. It's kind of a relaxed, Zen sort of job. After college, we both had the same desire to be independent. Wanted to be our own bosses. I wanted time to write. He wanted time to ski and go fishing. Wisdom says, "Never go into business with friends." We said, "Fuck that!" And we started a paint business.

I eventually planned to move, so we gave our company his last name. The license, bond and insurance, the legal and financial responsibilities were all in his name. Other than that, it was a partnership.

We had a ton of fun. We monkey'd around. We did what we wanted. We took off four months for winter so he could ski and I could travel. We did high-end custom work. We never advertised. We had no website. We just had a cellphone number, some business cards, and excellent word-of-mouth. After two years in business, we were awarded a contract to paint an enormous multi-million dollar dream-house.

We called the place Rattlesnake Ridge. It was constructed in the wrinkled hills that split Napa Valley from the Sacramento valley. The owner was a mega-rich developer. He leveled a hilltop and started erecting his custom villa. It took the stonemasons months to build his observation tower. Galileo's telescope would've fit in perfectly.

The construction site earned its deadly nickname. In the seven months we were there, workers caught or killed 56 rattlesnakes. I'm terrified of snakes... rattle or otherwise. My friend and partner knew how much I hated that dream-house. But that doesn't mean I wanted to burn it down.

Sometimes when you're properly fucked by Fate, you'll experience a sort-of shell-shocked numbness. My advice is... embrace that feeling. Hang onto it like it's gold. It's the best you're gonna feel for a long time because eventually you realize... this is really happening. And that moment, my friends, is worse than sucking sewage through a straw!

I expected the firemen to be rude. They'd been up all night putting out my wildfire. But the three fire marshals were nice. Each wore a well-meaning, non-ironic mustache. They told me the fire was 85% extinguished. The fire marshal from Solano County told me I'd started a 41-acre wildfire that burned the side of a mountain and most of the one next to it.

The detached garage was about the size of a three-bedroom suburban home. All that was left of it was collapsed into an enormous pile of blackened rubble, surrounded by crumbled adobe brick walls and topped with burnt-up ceiling timbers. Stepping on the still smoldering rubble, I pointed out to the fire marshals where we'd stored all of our volatile chemicals. And where the homeowners stored all their brand new ultra-expensive appliances. Then I showed them the door handles and hinges, all that was left of the twelve-foot tall authentic California Mission doors. Each antique door cost thousands of dollars. There used to be 18 of them.

I told the fire marshals we'd been using oil-based wood stain in the house for weeks. I told them how, every day, we inappropriately handled and stored the volatile chemicals. I showed them where we illegally stored 5-gallon buckets stuffed with highly-flammable oily rags, surrounded by all sorts of volatile chemicals, encircled by piles of canvas drop-cloths, and of course, the 18 authentic California Mission doors. They told me it might be impossible to make a more perfect and expensive starter kit for a structure fire. I knew we were supposed to have a metal firebox for the rags but we didn't have one.

The fire marshal from Yolo County had the best moustache of the three of them. When I was done answering questions and dooming my friend's future, he and his mustache told me, in 23 years of doing his job, I was the first person he'd ever met who told him the complete truth no matter how stupid it made me look.

He said, "Everyone lies to us. And then we always find out. Appreciate your honesty."

I said, "If I'm gonna ruin my best-friend's life... I might as well do it the way he wants me to... He said I should tell you guys the truth. He knows I'm a terrible liar."

According to the Napa County fire marshal's best guess, based on the information I'd just given them, the fire was started by sunlight. As the sun set rays of light were magnified through a plastic bag and ignited an oily rag. The fire burned slowly for most of the night. At some point around four a.m. the roof collapsed, creating a cloud of sparks and fiery debris, which landed on the dry summer grass. That's how the structure fire became a wildfire. An insomniac neighbor on the next mountain called 911. And that's what saved the dream-house from becoming charred timbers. Sometimes you get lucky.

The firemen said I was free to leave. It was time to go back to my life. But seriously, would you want to go back? I wanted someone else's life. Mine sucked because I'd just ruined my best friend's life.

When your world suddenly turns horrible...
Forget the past, it's gone.
Just try to get through the present as fast as you can.
Focus on the future where it might one day be better.

As I drove home, one thought banged around in my head.

Someone has to pay for this fire.

I called my friend as I drove. Not a fun call. But he didn't cuss. He didn't yell. He didn't even have a nasty tone. He's known for having a temper. And for knocking dudes out with one punch. But he sounded very matter-of-fact about the whole thing. He asked what I told the fire inspectors. I said the truth. He told me that was good because it was admissible in court. I knew, that he knew, he was fucked.

In business, a company must be insured in case anything goes wrong... like a fire. Before he left on his vacation, I asked my partner if he paid the bill for the insurance renewal. It was 150 dollars. He told me he'd pay it. Now, because he didn't mention it, I didn't need to ask if he'd sent in the renewal for the insurance. We discussed our next moves. Get a lawyer and wait for someone to contact us.

When the homeowner's insurance company finally called, they said it would cost $180,000 dollars to rebuild the garage. That's how big the garage was, how expensive the appliances were and, of course, they had to pay for the irreplaceable 18 authentic California Mission doors. 180 grand. That's enough money to buy like 22 houses in Detroit. I could live for the rest of my days on an island in the South Pacific for 180 grand. That's probably more than Charlie Sheen has spent on hookers and blow. Or maybe not.

I didn't have 180 grand. Figured that was it. Our friendship was done. Not because of the money. Because... How could he ever forgive me for fucking up his future, for crushing it with a burning mountain of debt?

I was responsible for everything while my friend was in Costa Rica. The fire was my fault. And most folks seemed to agree. The story people told was... my friend went on vacation, and while he was gone, I burned down 41 acres and a detached garage. He endured the same conversation whenever he ran into someone who'd heard the story of "the fire." Imagine you live in a small college town. Everyone knew the story. But after weeks of people blaming me for ruining his life, I never heard a single angry word from him.

The lawyer brokered a deal with the insurance company. It reduced my friend's financial burden. Since I was so honest, the fire marshals testified in our favor and then testified to help the homeowner's insurance company turn around and sue the homeowners. It got really messy at the end. When all was settled and done, my friend owed $50,000 dollars.

When we heard the final total, I apologized, but he stopped me. He said it wasn't my fault. I'd reminded him to renew the insurance and he didn't. So... it was no one's fault. Could you say that? It was one of the most remarkable things I've ever seen or heard.

Before I burned down a garage, 18 authentic California Mission doors and 41 acres of a mountainside, I didn't know how to forgive someone. $50,000 dollars later, my friend and partner taught me...

The best way to forgive someone is not to blame them.

Even if they ruin your future... don't blame them.

Blame the universe, dumb luck, the world's worst day... but not a person.

A few months ago, I went to my friend's wedding. We got really drunk at the reception. We had a good time. No one mentioned "the fire" or the $50,000 dollars. He's paid it off. It's in the past. For me, the fact I was even at his wedding, reminded me how crazy my friend is. He let a $50,000 dollar mountain of debt melt away like sugar in the rain. For a shit-talking ski bum who's been known to knock dudes out with one punch, and make them do the silly-walk before they collapse, the guy surprised me with his compassion.

Thanks to my most costly fuck-up yet, I learned from my friend the most valuable lesson:

If you don't blame anyone... you don't need to forgive anyone

Thought I'd share it with you... it kinda helps my friend get his money's worth.

* *

Ten Ways To Deal With Losing The One Person You Want

I don't know about you but I'd rather breakdance barefoot on broken glass than be rejected by the only person I want and desire. And yeah, I'm serious. The pain of losing the one you desire, the shame of being rejected, the self-doubt that sets in when you've been denied, they all teach you how emotional pain feels far worse than physical pain. And I'm not speaking metaphorically. I would gladly do bloody backspins before suffering heartbreak. The shitty thing is... we rarely get to choose.

I was once skateboarding down a super-steep hill in San Francisco when my board started to shake from speed-wobbles. Since I was going faster than cars were driving, when I finally crashed I shoved my hands down just as I hit the pavement. I thought I'd brace against the impact and then roll. Instead, I slid the length of numerous parked cars, and I sanded off all the skin from both hands. When I stopped sliding, my hands were smoking. I'm not kidding. Real smoke. That hurt like a motherfucker. Took weeks before I could use my hands. But I learned a broken body eventually heals. However, a broken heart... feels like it'll never be whole again. Just like with my skinless smoking hands, I speak from experience.

Recently, a woman I'd fallen for, she told me we have no future together. Ours was a long distance relationship- an affectionate friendship. And when I say long distance, there's an ocean and a continent between us. I'm such a naïve romantic I thought we could overcome such distance. We had the internet to help us. I believed love conquers all. But I learned it can't conquer the doubts of the one you love.

When she told me she didn't want do the long distance thing there really wasn't anything I could say. I offered to visit or move there to be with her. She felt if I relocated, the pressure would be unnatural, and she'd feel guilty if things didn't work out. I didn't understand this line of thinking. I still don't. But I don't blame her. I have to accept my heart knows what it wants while hers is unsure. And now, I must find a way to move on. After many long nights, lots of cussing and trips to the beach to let waves wash over me and wipe away my sadness, I wrote out this list. If you're dealing with heartbreak, it should help you, too.

1. **Don't Consider Your Loss... Think Of It As Their Loss**
   When another person makes it clear they don't want to be with you how else can you feel other than rejected? But this doesn't mean it's your loss. That's looking at the wrong side of the kiss. Rather than focus on how you don't get to know the softness of their lips. Remember they also miss out on the fullness of yours. And when you see it as their loss and not yours, it helps you maintain your

confidence. Too often we focus on what we're missing. But the one who walked away also misses out on something. You. That's their mistake. Feel bad for them. Pity their loss. If you can see it that way you keep your value and maintain your confidence. Just because they don't want you doesn't mean you're unworthy or unlovable.

2. **Accept The Fact You Have No Control Over Outcomes**
This one's a little more difficult. You may feel tempted to do things to change the outcome. You may think that if you slightly change who and how you are when you're around them, or maybe act or dress like someone they find more attractive, or perhaps somehow you can make them jealous, or maybe you can seduce them and romantically overwhelm them with the irresistibility of you. But let me tell you, none of that shit will work. You can't force things to happen. If you try all you end up doing is looking desperate. And no one likes desperate. It's unattractive. It casts a glaring spotlight on your fear you won't get what you want. It shows how you're willing to go to ridiculous lengths to be with the one you want. It suggests you don't believe it will happen, and that you're willing to do dumb shit to control the outcome. Instead, of playing games, accept you have no control over other people, no control over situations, and the only thing you can control is... yourself.

3. **Never Forget... ABC (Always Be Cool)**
Which brings us to the best thing you can do. Be cool like Fonzi. You know how The Fonz never acted emotionally stupid? He was unflappable. You have to be cool with what's happened. This will feel impossible. But if you remember #1 and #2, it gets

easier with each passing day. So during those times when you want to send them a text message, or "like" a Facebook status update, or you want to retweet something they posted, or maybe even call them up and "just check in," all of these would be motivated by the idea they'll see how funny/compatible/perfect for each other you are... so just don't. Remind yourself. ABC. Always Be Cool. Fonzi wouldn't drunk text someone. He knows it's their loss. And that's your new job. Keep your cool.

4. **Allow Yourself A Moment to Be Sad (But Don't Feel Sorry For Yourself)**
Now, unlike an imaginary character like The Fonz, you'll have moments of weakness, moments of sadness, moments when tears wet your cheeks and there's not much you can do to stop them. Don't even try. There's nothing wrong with crying, there's nothing wrong with being sad. The only danger is when you let those feelings linger too long. Give yourself moments, days, maybe even weeks of sadness. But eventually, if you continue to dwell on your sadness, you're just feeling sorry for yourself. And if you need some perspective take a trip down to any burn center or trauma unit if you want or need an undeniable reminder of why you shouldn't feel sorry for yourself.

5. **Distract Yourself**
If you're having trouble, forgetting about the one you lost, the best thing to do is distract yourself. Visit people who do care about you. Spend time with folks who bring you joy. Take up a new hobby. Find a new passion. Try something you've always been curious about but have yet to ever do. If you have the time and money, travel. If you don't yet have the time and money, then let literature and

films carry you away. Especially, things that make you laugh. Treat comedy like medicine and when the blues pay you a visit, let laughter be your antidote. Watch old favorites and seek out new funny films as well. The key is not to dwell on you, your past, or your lost future. Distract yourself with positivity. Laughter, like truth, will set you free.

6. **Stop Beating Yourself Up**
   Another key to fighting the temptation to dwell on how you feel is to stopbeating yourself up. It's not your fault. Sometimes we don't get what we want. That's just how it goes. So accept this sad piece of wisdom and recognize there probably wasn't anything you could've done differently.But for the sake of argument, let's say there was. Well, there's nothing you can do about it now. So let it go. Unless you have a time machine, all you can do is learn from the past. You can't fix it.

7. **Give Up The Idea It Might Work Out Eventually**
   Another thing that's super-important is you'll need to give up the idea things might work out, eventually. Yes, none of knows what will happen in the future. But that doesn't mean you should use that as an argument to hold out hope. Maybe the one who got away will realize what they're missing and come back, but don't hang on to such a silly life preserver of hope. Start swimming. Focus on right now. They're gone. So act like they're gone and don't wait for them to come back. If for some reason they do come back, let it be a pleasant surprise. In the meantime, live your life.

8. **Stop Comparing Yourself to Others**
   You may find in your darkest moments you're comparing yourself to others, and their happiness

feels like knives between your ribs and darts stabbing you in your eyes. We all love to compare ourselves to others, but just don't. You never know how others really feel. You think you can see how unfair life is, how another couple is just so goddamn happy, and how they have the perfect life and it's just so horribly unfair. But you never know. Maybe driving home, a month from now, one of the people in that perfectly happy couple is killed by a drunk driver. And the survivor is left to mourn. Don't assume anything. And don't compare yourself. It's a waste of your time.

9. **Don't Be Embarrassed... Be Proud**
   You may feel pathetic or pitiful, that you're obviously an unlovable loser. But you're not. You're just unlucky. Don't be embarrassed because you put your heart out there and someone else said, "No thanks." Be proud you were willing to love. There are far too many people in this world who will never be as brave as you were. And those people have almost zero chance of ever knowing love because they're not trying and failing. You may have failed this time, but anyone who's ever wanted anything in this world most likely had their share of disappointments and setbacks. So be proud you risked your heart. And get ready to do it again... that's the only way you'll find real and lasting love. Don't pull a Bogey in Casablanca and shut your heart off from the world, in the hopes that it never gets broken again. It took a team of screenwriters to get his character, Rick, to open his heart back up. You don't have that luxury. Just be proud of yourself and keep trying. Love is worth a little pain along the way.

10. **Trust Your Future Will Surprise You... And Move**

On

Finally, here's one other piece of advice from Hollywood. William Goldman, the screenwriter who gave us "The Princess Bride" and a number of other great movies, is often quoted for saying a great truth about Hollywood, but it applies to life in general. *"Nobody Knows Anything."* These three little words hold so much wisdom. And you, my friend, may think you know how things will turn out, or what to expect in your future, or that you know what you've learned from your past, but then one little event occurs or a realization surfaces that proves everything you thought you knew is wrong. Have faith in the great weirdness of life and trust your future will surprise you. Let the promise of that premise help you to move on. Don't wait for the future to happen. You still have to get out there and do things to find the love and happiness you deserve. But trust that you never know what tomorrow holds in its hands. And move with eager and open eyes towards the rising sun of tomorrow and perhaps, you'll get lucky. The future will always surprise you. Sometimes, it's shitty and you'll find heartbreak waiting around the bend. Other times, the surprise is more wonderful than you could have designed it.

Wesley Snipes said always bet on black.

I'm here to remind you to always bet on the great weirdness of life.

Just stay open to love.

* *

How To Not Hate All The Happy Couples

T oday's one of those days the universe is fucking with me. Wherever I go my eyes run smack into yet another kissing couple. Warm weekend days in Los Angeles bring out the lovers. It's like how Kelis and her milkshake bring all the boys to the yard. It's one of those moth-to-flame scenarios. Los Angeles really knows how to do Spring. Everywhere your eyes focus flowers are in full bloom. The weather feels warm but not yet too hot. The flesh-revealing outfits of pedestrians are sexy in a way that makes horny drivers risk car accidents. It's a perfect season for romance and love.

Earlier today, I was in traffic in West Hollywood, waiting at a red light. Two dudes on bicycles were standing at the same stoplight, also waiting for it to change colors. As if on cue, they leaned toward each other and started to kiss. Embarrassing as it is to admit I sneered at the sight of them. Then I felt eyes on me. When I turned my head, I caught the driver in the car next to mine, staring at me. He looked disgusted with me. His face pinched in the same way I was glowering at the two kissing lovers.

Quick to do the math, I guessed what his story must be. I figured the other driver assumed I was some certified homophobic asshole. I always hate how my face is so easy to read. Freeway billboards aren't as easy to read as my face. I wanted to drop my window and explain to the driver I didn't care a whit that two guys were lip-locking at the stoplight. I don't lump people into groups and then hate on them. I always dislike people individually. I wasn't mad because two gay dudes were kissing. I was mad because I wasn't kissing.

Basically, I was envious of their affection for each other. I knew with the same certainty one knows rain will get you wet, I had no one to kiss and my lips would remain dry for the conceivable future. Jealousy gnawed on my heart with the ferocity of a starving rat. And just like how my girl Fiona Apple sings it, "hunger hurts."

Those bicycle-riding lovers could've been two grey-haired geezers swapping spit and I would've sneered at them. Luckily, the two kissing dudes couldn't see me. Only the other driver caught sight of my ugly face. But I couldn't explain to him how I was solely disgusted with myself. The two dudes were just a mirror and made it impossible for me to ignore the fact I had no love to call my own. I'd been depriving myself the ecstasy of such a spontaneous kiss. Their sweet love moment made me feel all the more alone, sitting at that red light on a warm spring day in May.

If you look at the world as a reflection of your state of affairs, you will experience moments like these. You will say to yourself in that hideous serpentine voice of envy, "Fuck that-I don't need to see that shit." It doesn't really matter what "that shit" is, all you care is, it's not you, or it's not yours. This is a mistake we all make. Just like how children get upset when they see other kids enjoying bigger cookies than the one they got for snack-time. For some reason we tend to focus on how our cookie isn't as large as the cookie others are enjoying. And then we get mad. It may not be love that upsets you but rather it's the fact others have more money, power, or prestige. It doesn't really matter. It's not the cookie but the comparison that triggers jealousy.

It's exceedingly difficult not to measure our lives by contrasting our circumstances against others. One of the hardest things you ever do on a regular day-to-day basis is ignore the temptation to compare yourself to someone else. It's just so easy. And it's so misleading. How do you know anyone else's circumstances? Those two guys on their bikes might've been kissing because it was the last day they'd ever spend together before one of them returned to Portugal.

Rarely, if ever, do we detect the truth. Yet we think we know what's going on when it's happening right in front of our faces. We tell ourselves the story of what we see. And we're almost always wrong. There's usually something we're missing. Yet this doesn't stop us from having an emotional reaction because there aren't many stronger or faster feelings than jealousy, which is usually followed by the anger that courses through us as we "see" how everyone else is doing better than we are.

We compare ourselves so often and so easily a casual observer would think we actually gained something from it. But on the real, nope, we're just seeing the world as a reflection of our mental/emotional state. A person only knows what they know. And there's just so much each of us doesn't know. We rarely get it right when we guess. Which makes it a completely useless waste of your limited time on this garden we call Earth.

The guy in the car was most likely wrong about me. And it's just as likely I was wrong about him. Maybe I reminded him of some college roommate he despised for sleeping with his ex-girlfriend and he hadn't even noticed I was sneering at the two kissing guys on the bikes. And those two dudes enjoying a sunny day in May... maybe theirs was a secret affair, and there was no beautiful love involved at all, and instead it was a moment of escape and stolen romance. I don't know. We never really know.

If, like me, you catch sight of what appears to be a happy couple, and their love makes you feel lonely, unwanted and passed over, the only truth in that moment is, you feel alone. Instead of chalking it up to the gross unfairness of life, do something about that shit. And rather than swallow any more bitterness or resentment, focus on the positive, think about how you can find someone who wants to wet your lips with kisses. Anger and jealousy won't help you find happiness. They'll push it away. So fuck all that noise. Reject the tendency to compare. And find what you want. You deserve beauty and love, too.

* *

Why Women Are Sexy... To A Man Like Me

I 've been thinking a lot about why certain aspects of a woman are sexy. Obviously, I don't expect anyone to agree with me. And I hope you don't expect me to agree with you. We all have our individual preferences. These are just the qualities I like and desire. They're not universal. They're not better than what you like. They're not what all guys like. These are the aspects of a woman that take my breath away. Maybe you prefer a woman's feet while I prefer the shape of her ankles-because, I do. A woman's ankle is as specific and sexy as her laugh. Yet, a woman's feet and ankles should be equally appreciated. And don't worry, this isn't some wolfish rumination on a woman's body and why her various parts are sexy. To me, the valley of a woman's clavicle is as sexy as the agility of her curiosity. Her integrity turns me on as much as her pierced nipples.

Let's start with something that is rather obvious but often overlooked for its sex appeal. I'm talking about the explosion of a woman's smile across her face when she's so giddy it feels like her chest might split open and her heart will flutter away like a butterfly high on PCP. You know, those moments when you know a laugh isn't the right response but it just takes hold of every fiber of your being and your rippling with the dopamine rush of unstoppable giggles. Seeing a woman, at home in her skin, yet bursting at the seams with surprise makes me feel about as alive as I assume jumping out of a perfectly good airplane feels for a skydiver. No bullshit. Making a woman laugh turns me on. Especially, when she shouldn't laugh, like when she's mad.

Another underappreciated small pleasure I find that reduces me to wordlessness is the smell of a woman's neck when I draw close enough to kiss her or whisper something in her ear. Doesn't matter if she's been working out and she's all sweaty, if she's been driving all day and she feels crusty, if she's just woken up and she feels ready to shower, or if she's camping and thinks she smells like a bear's ass. I like the smell of a woman's neck. It emits wisps of the aroma of that particular woman. I also enjoy the smell of her hair, but too often women use so many hair products, I wind up with the nose-bite of perfumed shampoo, hair treatments, and the fragrance of conditioner that combine to bury the pheromones of her scent. But a woman's neck is the reason I cherish slow dancing at a wedding (and outside of weddings how often do we slow dance? Damn shame).

While we're discussing dancing, this reminds me... a woman's hips and the curve that descends from her ribcage down to her pelvis is the place in this world where my hands are their happiest. A woman doesn't need to be skinny; in fact, I find it's better if she has more than less. Let's say we're standing on a pier, watching the sun fall into the sea, my hand resting on her waist, erotic thoughts charge through me like the waves breaking against the shore. It's the soft feel of what makes her a woman. Her pelvis is unlike mine, and it pleasures me to feel her foreign femininity against my fingers.

Moving from hips to the way they swing when a woman walks, seems a natural segue, so let's consider the cadence of her movement. Given the geometry of a woman and her lower center of gravity, most women seem to sway as they move through the world. And if she possesses confidence in herself, it shows up in her walk the same way you can spot it in the shine in her eyes. Doesn't matter if she walks towards me or away, watching the woman I desire walk gives birth to erotic thoughts that would make a pornographer blush. There's little that's sexier to me than the way a confident woman strides through the world. She can be slow and seductive like how Sade moves, or quietly strong and defiant like Julia Ormond, she can be openly sexy and flirtatiously playful like Salma Hayek in just about any movie she's ever been in, or she can somehow float the way Ingrid Bergman moves through *Notorious* and *Casablanca*. If she's the one for me, watching her walk is one of those moments when everything seems just right in the world.

There are guys who are leg-men. A woman's calf makes them hungry like the wolf salivating at the sight of a plump chicken. That's not my thing. I get why the sloping curves of a woman's calf might bring out their inner beast.

Legs are sexy, no doubt. But for me, the back of a woman's knees houses the mysteries I could spend days in bed trying to decipher. The tendons and ligaments beneath the skin give the back of the knee its contours, the nature of the knee gives it the necessary indent for the knee to bend, and the flesh found there is so rarely seen it's like a surprise you discover behind the hill of a meadow where flowers give way to grass and despite the lack of color, the grass is as soft under the feet as the flowers are a treat for the eyes. The back of a woman's knee is often a place where on a warm day she glistens with sweat. And if you know anything about perspiration, you know it transmits the warm aroma and pheromones particular to the woman you desire. With tiny kisses, I'll consider the back of her knee, and with happy fingers I like to feel the specific curves and valley of that hidden joint.

Moving from body to mind, a woman who makes great conversation can keep me enthralled until the sun pokes its head back up over the horizon to start a new day. And there's something undeniably sexy about the surprise of a far-roaming and wide-reaching conversation with a woman who delights in her own curiosity and considers all the angles and back alleys of a subject. A woman who can exhaust the ears of most men is the sort I seek out. The more opinionated she is, the better. The more ready she is to argue her view, the more likely I will desire her contrary mind, even if I never change views and agree with her. Smart women prove how one's mind is our greatest erogenous zone. A woman's mind often turns me on more than her décolletage.

The laughter of a woman will linger in my mind like a riddle; the sort one puzzles over for the rest of their life. I long to know how I can hear that mellifluous laugh erupt from her again and again and again. The funny thing is, I don't care if she giggles like a girl, or brays like a jenny, as long as she's genuinely laughing I delight in the sound of her chortles, guffaws, titters, and snorts. I like to hear a woman when she's unhinged. Too often, in my opinion, a woman is convinced she should be concerned with what others think and consequently, she girdles herself in ways that seem unnatural. And thus, when she loses her careful self-restraint and laughs, I desire her all the more. And if she has a wicked sense of humor, a hint of darkness in her laugh, I feel even closer her to her heart, because in my chest beats a dark heart, too.

Eyes. Nothing and I mean nothing is as sexy as a woman's eyes. This is why the world's traditions that require a woman to veil herself but allow her eyes to be seen always make me wonder what's the point. Sure, I can't see her ass but if her eyes bore into my soul, I will desire her the same way Casanova chased skirts. A woman's eyes are more than mere windows on the soul, they are worlds in and of themselves. I long to dive in and swim in the pools of her blue, to memorize those oceans of her green to learn every micro-current of the lakes of her brown. There are a million little ways an eye communicates. There is a vocabulary each woman teaches you with just her eyes. I savor the nuances of this language of her eyes, not only does my heart draw nearer to her, but my mind grows feverish with anticipation. One look from across a crowded room can be as clearly flirtatious and sexy as a love letter.

This last thing is a superficial trifle. But it is a matter of a woman's choice. Her underwear. Why something as cliché as underwear? Well, despite all my romanticism, I'm still a dude. I lust for a woman's mind, I delight in her laughter, her eyes and her confidence render me clumsy with my words, but I crave the chance to touch her skin. Her underwear is the last border between her and nakedness. To conceal is better than to reveal. We all know this. Which means underwear is the final frontier, the last revelation before flesh and thus a woman's underwear is the sexiest thing she ever wears. Sometimes, I'll take my time undressing a woman, maybe not unhook her bra and just push her panties to the side for us to enjoy our afternoon quickie. Going somewhere formal, I might ask her to wear garters and stockings like a bride on her wedding day. And on hot summer days, I love to see a woman in something silly yet sexy like striped knee-high socks... and only striped knee-high socks. I have no explicit favorites. It all works for me as long as it works for her.

When a woman feels desired, that's the first step in the dance of foreplay. A man's sexuality, like bow-and-arrow, pulls taut with tension, is targeted, and climaxes with the joy of release. A woman's sexuality, like a sandcastle, is delicate, playful, constructive and yet beautifully impermanent. It is the architecture of her attitude that makes a woman sexy... to a man like me.

* *

Love Is All Around… No, Really It Is

I'm single and with each passing day it feels like I've carved another notch in my bedpost, a pattern of mounting evidence I'll always be alone. Mostly, I think this because I'm something of an odd duck. How many women want a wandering freelance writer with aquamarine hair who likes surfing at dawn, tequila bars at sunset, watching avante-garde French movies, reading about the cosmos and believes a long walk with a camera is an awesome Saturday? Not exactly husband material, I know. But one thought sustains my hope I won't always be alone, and it's a simple one. It's applies to you and everyone you know. It's millennia old, it's Latin, but it's undeniably true, in the way all lasting aphorisms hold timeless wisdom:

Audentes Fortuna Iuvat!

Luck favors the bold. That's all I tell myself to keep going. I don't care about the numbers, the likelihoods, the social trends or what the patterns suggest... blind stubborn hope and boldness work for me. I play love like it's the goddamn lottery. And Jesus tap-dancing Christ... I know, I must sound like the sort of annoyingly optimistic dumb-bunny you'd meet at a convention of romance novelists. The kind you know is going home to a cat, or twelve. And seeing it all spelled out, the words stand there like an indictment-*blind stubborn hope.* That's the attitude of naïve hopeless romantics. But that's not me. I'm a *hopeful* romantic. It's an important distinction, and mostly, because I worked for it.

I didn't start out this way. I converted to delusional optimism after years and years of pessimism. I've been cynical about life since I first learned to read. Seeing how the world works didn't exactly imbue me with much confidence there were lots of good reasons to get excited about growing up. I had no burning desire to become an adult. It looked like a hypocritical, self-conscious way to be and to my young eyes the world of adults resembled some sort of dangerous playground with a terrible maintenance record.

It was really difficult to become optimistic. It took me years. There's no way I'm going back. The cynics may be right more often than I am, but it's a terribly boring way to live. They have no use for magic or wonder or the sweetness of dumb luck. Insurance salesmen are cynical. Corporate accountants are cynical. A career politician is cynical. Children, on the other hand, aren't cynical. Guess I'm standing with the kids on this one. I know cynics would say I'm like a junkie for love. But really, who gives a shit what they think? I've lived both ways and there's no comparison. Sure, it's harder to be optimistic, especially if it doesn't come naturally, but optimism means you move towards things rather than away from them. Some of us need that shift. Otherwise our lives are a series of near-escapes and avoidance.

I know exactly how a tendency to over-think things drives one to the solace of cynicism. One day, I got sick of being right about people and situations. It only limited what I did, who I spent time around and where I went. I was stupidly trying to protect myself from life's bullshit, which by the way is impossible. How is avoidance a good way to lead your life (unless we're talking about things like uranium, carbon monoxide or the paparazzi)?

I stopped playing the percentages. Life ain't a hand of blackjack. I stopped trying to be smart about everything. I wasn't enjoying my life much because I wasn't risking much and I wasn't very engaged with others. By thinking so much about the future, I was spending more and more time hanging out with my fears. By trying to protect myself from what might happen I was motivated by avoidance rather than encouraging myself to go boldly after what I desired-this is a terrible way to spend your days.

Rather than soar and dive like a hungry hawk hunting field mice, now I flit and float like a drunken butterfly. I rarely look before I leap. I just go. I trust I'll make the best of things. Guess you could say I started to trust myself. Apparently, I didn't use to. Now, I lean into tomorrow with the unquestioned belief good shit will happen. Often, on a day-to-day basis nothing remarkable happens. But I rather childishly remain enthusiastic about the next day, and the day after that. Kids get it. Life is generally awesome. Boring people, fearful people and unimaginative people miss that great truth. Yes, there's pain and suffering, but there's also Charlie Parker, fireworks, mint chocolate chip ice cream, the artwork of Jean-Michel Basquiat, the scent of a woman's hair, the contagious grin of a 100-yeard old man, and the 4th Movement of Beethoven's Ninth Symphony.

Once I stopped fretting about the future I was free to fully enjoy moments of life like never before, and now I let things like hope and dumb luck guide my path through life. The best side effect of this polar shift in perspective was I found love is all around. No shit. Just like the cliché instructs. It sucks how clichés relate to our lives. As kids we learn them because everyone says them and they're somewhat helpful. Then as a teen or twentysomething we hate clichés, they're things to explode and prove wrong. Only later do we find out they became clichés for a reason. They hold some truth. And when I say clichés I don't mean like fashion trends or the lame sameness of sitcoms, I mean our cultural clichés, those sayings that represent the common wisdom on a subject. "*Love is all around*" is one of those clichés.

Love is the currency that motivates us, its absence perverts our view of the world, and its presence is the engine of our most worthwhile human interactions. John Lennon was right. Love is all you need. Bankers and power brokers believe money makes the world go 'round.

They're wrong. Just like water, money is important, but love makes the merry-go-round.

If you feel alone, seek out someone to share your world. It took me ages to figure out love isn't about acquisition, it's about exchange. That's also why looking for love can sometimes feels like trying to find a pearl in a pool of manure. You're looking for a treasure amongst a mass of shit you don't need. But that's not really how it works. The world isn't all shit and the pearl isn't some lost treasure you need to find. Sometimes love finds you and it's all just a matter of dumb luck. We often think long and hard about the big decisions in life, but when looking at a life in retrospect it's often the little decisions that change our lives. The decision to get Mexican food for lunch may end up affecting your life far more than the decision of which college to attend or which home to buy or rent.

I have friends who met at a party. She was back from a trip to Bali where she'd contracted a tropical disease that tried to kill her. She fought it off for months and she was still near-death with sickness when she went back to law school. Other than to attend class or visit the library she rarely left her house. She was just clawing and crawling through each day. At the end of the quarter, a friend told her she needed to get out and just have a beer-she declined. Her friend demanded she go.

At the luau-themed party, already somewhat tired and unused to going out, she sat down on the floor. From across the room she saw an orange rolling toward her. She looked up and saw a guy sitting in an inflatable canoe filled with ice and fruit for the luau. He grinned at her. She smiled back. Mostly, because she knew she'd just met her husband. And she was right. I was the minister at their wedding. They now have three awesome boys and she's a lawyer that gets mentioned on television by Bill Maher. So, yeah... sometimes that happens. You go somewhere you don't want to go, sit down on the floor and you meet the love of your life.

As my friends' love story indicates the hand of luck is invisible. You never know when you might find someone who wants to play the game of give-and-take. Love, like most of life, is a paradox. It slips from grip when you grasp for it, it squirms away when you try to define it, and love will run off when you try to make it do your bidding, but if you hold it like a bird in your hand, if you stay open to its surprise, it often shows up when you least expect it. You might find it at your roommate's sister's birthday party, or you might find it at a carwash, or you might find it at the airport. And wouldn't that be perfectly ironic? Finding love as you wait to claim your baggage? Life's funny that way. I keep an eye out for the orange rolling towards me because you just never know. Sometimes, great love stories begin with a rare tropical disease.

* *

Acknowledgments

Stephanie Georgopulos, Brandon Scott Gorrell, Stephen Tully Dierks: *for being kickass editors and hardworking, thoughtful humans*

Meghan Underwood: *my favorite person on the planet, only sister and first audience*

Claudia Burnett: *for her unwavering belief in me since birth*

Dora Moutot: *for her inspiration and partnership and for broadening my world*

Lyle and VerJean Conard: *for their constant support*

Pearl Cleage: *mentor, friend and hero to a young writer*

Zaron Burnett Jr.: *for introducing me to words and their magic*

Bruce Talamon: *for his generosity and talent*

Langston Edwards: *lifelong friend and world's best/funniest lawyer*

Pam Mari, Victoria Cerati & Widgen Neagley: *my favorite teachers, all of whom instilled a love of great writing and the notion I had a voice worth expressing*

Mink Choi: *for being a badass book producer, for all her hours of labor and her brilliant design work putting this together. I'm forever indebted to you for making my first one such a beautiful book.*

About the Writer

Photo by Bruce Talamon

Zaron Burnett III is a writer and filmmaker and rumored to be the illegitimate lovechild of Otis Redding and Frida Kahlo. However, all indications suggest he started this rumor, which is especially ridiculous since Frida Kahlo was incapable of having children and both of them died long before he was born. What is known is he was raised in Georgia and Northern California, and on more than one occasion has expressed a strong desire to be a dolphin on his next vacation. He believes in love, sex, drugs and the multiverse theory, particularly the notion that amongst the many possible realities, there exists one where he is the President of Fiji, but only took the job for the good surfing.

www.ingramcontent.com/pod-product-compliance
Lightning Source LLC
Chambersburg PA
CBHW031451070426
42452CB00038B/702